WHAT PEOPLE ARE SAYING

WALL STREET TO THE WELL

Transformation is a key word in our lives. Over the last fifty years in media, the most meaningful has been the last twenty-plus years with Education Media Foundation as CEO of K-LOVE and Air1 Radio Networks. I have been so encouraged and touched by the millions of stories listeners have shared. In Stu Fuhlendorf's book, *Wall Street to the Well*, God shows who He is and how His glory transforms and restores His children—all through His love and grace. Stu captures how God impacts even the most rebellious and underserving to a place of redemption and peace. This book will edify and encourage anyone who reads it. Enjoy.

—*Mike Novak*
CEO K-LOVE and Air1 Radio

Wall Street to the Well is a riveting account of one man's journey towards relational, emotional and spiritual wholeness. This is not a book of quick-fixes, pat answers and quick resolutions. It is a story of a patient God coming alongside an ambitious and flawed man who at his worst is just like us and at his best is the person we'd hope to be. This book is for those who aspire for all life has to offer in all its fullness. Let Stu help show you the way.

—*Eric Swanson*
Leadership Network, Co-Author of *The Externally Focused Church* and *To Transform a City*

My relationship with Stu Fuhlendorf started over twenty years before he was a Christian. From the time of our first business endeavor, to today, his life has been re-directed from business executive to pastor. *Wall Street to the Well* is a fascinating story of his metamorphosis. But the book isn't about an unfulfilled quest, it's about a journey ending in finding true meaning. Stu's life has been transformed because of his love of the gospel, and his relationship with Jesus Christ. Anybody who is interested in examining why they may be feeling discontented, in good times or bad should read Stu's book. We can all use a dose of encouragement through the trials, tribulations and struggles that life throws our way. This book will do just that.

—*Dick Monfort*
Owner/Chairman & Chief Executive Officer, Colorado Rockies Baseball Club

God chooses to show us more of Himself in the lives of those He transforms. I cannot think of another man where I have seen God's long-suffering, sovereignty, and love more vivid than in Stu Fuhlendorf. In his book, *Wall Street to the Well*, God's power and individualized care are displayed in Stu's riveting story. You will walk away with such joy in seeing how God can take someone who was once an adversary to now being an advocate for Him. This remarkable story will show the power of God and how the love of Christ can permeate any status or situation.

—*Josh Weidmann*
Senior Pastor of Grace Chapel and author of
Honest to God

Many years ago, I was truly blessed to be introduced to Stu in my darkest hour, at the pinnacle of desperation, with the uncertainty of family and faith all colliding at the same time. I turned more and more to a bottle rather than the real answer, a relationship with God! Stu's understanding, love and guidance over the years have been inspirational and at times given me the strength to keep going, even when doubts crept in. Though I knew part of his story, after reading *Wall Street to the Well* I am reinvigorated with the hope and faith that sustains through good times and bad.

—*Mike Milender*
Founding Member, Milender White
Construction Company

The God who turns ashes into beauty, mourning into joy, and despair into praise is alive and well. If you have any doubts, read this amazing story by my friend Stu. If your life is broken—or you are holding on to hope for a lost spouse, loved one, or friend—*Wall Street to the Well* will encourage you with the promises and pathways of the God who restores a broken life to a trophy of grace.

—*Daniel Henderson*
President, Strategic Renewal International and author
of *Transforming Prayer* and *Old Paths, New Power*

One can write arguing against the fallacy of atheism, agnosticism, hedonism, and the autonomous enlightened person based on theoretical research. It is also possible to write about the destructive end result and vanity of materialism, fame, wealth, and unguarded immorality without life experience. What makes Stu's book mind captivating to the reader is the narration of real life. *Wall Street to the Well* is a witness of a transformed individual who attests the vanity of worldly pursuit, the depravity of human beings, the mercy and redemption of God, the power of commitment demonstrated through his wife, and the pursuit and love of God to an unlovable person. Like an action movie, each chapter leads you to the next with great suspense. The end is a glorious victory, amazing grace, complete restoration of life and satisfaction that no earthly dream is able to offer. I highly recommend it to all who are in search of meaning in this precarious life.

—*Dr. Alex Mekonnen*
Professor of Missions, Regent University

Wall Street to the Well is a must-read for anyone who has been blessed with success yet struggles with self-sufficiency and pride. Stu Fuhlendorf shares his own powerful story of being a man who had it all but didn't need God. His was a journey of peaks and valleys. Along the way he encountered a God who pursued him, shook his world, and changed him from the inside out.

—*Mike Romberger*
President and Chief Executive Officer, Mount Hermon
Christian Conference Center

For those of you who think you know the definition of a successful (business) person, think again. In this fallen world of indulgences and riches . . . all is vanity. Pastor Stu has already discovered what some of us are still seeking . . . to place riches in heaven and not of this World. *Wall Street to the Well* chronicles the journey through his life, the triumphs, the tribulations, the transformation. This personal story of a life transformed gives you a life-changing perspective.

—*John Karas*
Retired Lockheed Martin, Vice President and
General Manager

Wall Street to the Well is an excellent and moving testimony about God's sovereign grace and the love of Jesus Christ our Lord, lavished upon a 'prodigal son' addicted and sold to power, money and pleasures. Stu Fuhlendorf's personal story will provide invincible hope for numerous people who are battling with the question of true meaning and purpose of their lives. This book is a must read for anyone that is searching and seeking for eternal values and causes in their everyday suffering and struggle.

—*Dr. Sung Wook Chung*
Professor of Christian Theology, Denver Seminary

I have witnessed many stories of lives changed by Christ on the impoverished streets of our cities. My friend Stu's book, *Wall Street to the Well,* will captivate you with a different but equally incredible faith journey that began not among the marginalized, but in the lavish lifestyle of corporate America, living as a former public company CFO and hardened self-confident atheist. His radical transformation by Christ offers a heartfelt testament to the power of the Gospel that cannot be denied.

—*Tom Leavitt*
Denver Rescue Mission, Director of Family Services

Stories are the currency of our culture and this one is rich. With refreshing candor and authenticity Stu brings the reader right into his childhood, boardroom, marriage, relationships, and calls it like he sees it. There are no formulas and quick fixes for deep hurt or addictions, only a Savior can save, and Stu reminds us of that in this page turner!

—*Daryl Heald*
Founder, Generosity Path

WALL STREET
to the WELL

A Story of Transformation from Fortune to Faith

STUART FUHLENDORF

ILLUMIFY MEDIA GLOBAL
Littleton, Colorado

WALL STREET
to the WELL

Unless otherwise noted, all Scripture references are from The Holy Bible,
English Standard Version. ESV® Text Edition: 2016. Copyright © 2001
by Crossway Bibles, a publishing ministry of Good News Publishers.
Scripture marked NIV is from the Holy Bible, New International
Version®, NIV® Copyright ©1973, 1978, 1984, 2011 by Biblica, Inc.®
Used by permission. All rights reserved worldwide.

The views and opinions expressed in this book are those of the author and
do not necessarily reflect the official policy or position of
Illumify Media Global.

Published by
Illumify Media Global
www.IllumifyMedia.com
"Write. Publish. Market. *SELL!*"

Library of Congress Control Number: 2018966333

Paperback ISBN: 978-1-949021-43-1
eBook ISBN: 978-1-949021-44-8

Printed in the United States of America

To my wife, Trish,
and my son and daughter, Erich and Hannah

CONTENTS

FOREWORD

STU FUHLENDORF and I first met when he was the pastor of evangelism and outreach at a megachurch in Colorado. We quickly became friends and trusted confidants. Over the years, I've observed firsthand how his background and life journey has given him instant credibility. And that's because his powerful story gives him an opportunity to empathize with others on a similar path.

Theoretical or theological musings are merely academic, if they do not acknowledge the practical, real-life side—both positive and negative. Stu understands this profoundly, due primarily to his personal experiences. He has had his share of ups and downs and has come to realize how the highs can be illusive and fleeting and the lows can be transformative. In the following pages of this book, Stu shares the life-changing lessons he's learned from his life failures and successes with clarity and wisdom. As a result, his book is filled with reflections relatable to anyone from anywhere.

While doing some strategic consulting work at the church Stu was pastoring, he demonstrated his genuine passion for the gospel of Jesus Christ. He is driven to communicate the transformative nature of the gospel and use whatever biblical means available to see lives changed and souls saved. It's evident that Stu's fascinating journey, eventually leading him to become a stellar evangelist, has been driven by the Holy Spirit using his successes and failures and his joys and sufferings to create in him an unending desire to see people become followers of Christ. There's no doubt Stu is deeply concerned for the eternal destiny of those all around him, both inside and outside the church.

This like-minded passion brought us together with a common purpose to see lives transformed, in a meaningful and lasting way—one life at a time. We were eager to inspire, equip, and mobilize every believer we could influence to become the instrument of God's hand in inviting others to become followers of Christ too. During our time working together, we initiated a cutting-edge evangelism strategy which included training staff and the congregation to engage in building genuine friendships with people who were far from God, interviewing non-Christians during weekend services in order to best learn how they prefer to be approached, and launching spiritual discussion groups designed specifically for people exploring tough spiritual questions. These, along with similar initiatives, became the foundation of our "One Life" approach where every believer within the church prayerfully identified one person they felt God was leading them to reach. And Stu was the leader overseeing this whole process. And he led well.

Stu reaches people effectively because he authentically cares about people. Each life matters to him. And that humble attitude is consistent in him because, by God's grace, it has been shaped by where he has come from, the redemption he has found, and where he is heading now. The destructive patterns of his life have become great reminders that drive his kind interactions with others. Stu has become seasoned in how he wisely expresses the reasons for his faith in Christ by appealing to the rational, personal, emotional, and spiritual aspects of faith. Stu's discernment, magnified by his personal experiences, shines brightly throughout his book. You can't miss it!

Wall Street to the Well is a personal memoir that reveals where real purpose and significance is found. It is a fascinating reflection on the destructive depravities of this world, how a loving God turns judgment into mercy and grace, the power of a godly and committed wife and family, and the unmitigated grace of God in his pursuit of all people—even the most undeserving. Stu's book is a compelling read, like a suspense novel building tension from chapter to chapter. You'll be captivated to discover how God has worked throughout Stu's life with amazing grace—a tribute to God's glory.

— **Garry Poole,** author of *Seeker Small Groups and*
The Complete Book of Questions

PREFACE

My story is a profound example of how any effort to delight in God must be empowered by God himself. All other effort consistently comes up short. This book is my testimony of God's work and spiritual empowerment that has transformed my life. In speaking about the importance of personal testimonies, Revelation 12:11 says, "And they have conquered him by the blood of the Lamb and by the word of their testimony, for they loved not their lives even unto death."

When Jesus encountered the Samaritan woman at the well in John 4, he offered her the living water of eternal life. He didn't care about her reputation, accomplishments or possessions, and he didn't care about her ethnicity or appearance. Jesus pursued her. Two thousand years later, Jesus is still the one who pursues.

ACKNOWLEDGMENTS

I AM immensely thankful for the work of Michael J. Klassen and Illumify Media Global on my memoir. Michael saw the value of my story in a way that only a publisher and an ordained pastor could. In an effort to live my life as a Christian to the glory of God who magnifies the worthiness of Christ, the message of this book is central. Michael's work was crucial in conveying the message.

Trish became a Christian before me, and for the next eight years she prayed, counseled, and cried for me; she sweated and suffered with a difficult man in an unequally yoked marriage. Throughout the suffering and purification, she remained faithful and relentless in her love. Her perseverance and determination, with God's strength, helped her survive a tough decade of marriage, during which she was a model godly woman. Some days are still tough, but we have a blessed marriage of thirty-one years. And she continues to be a model godly woman today. Proverbs 31:28-29 reminds me of Trish: "Her children rise up and call her blessed; her husband also, and he praises her: 'Many women have done excellently, but you surpass them all.' "

Erich and Hannah have lived a life full of ups and downs, mainly driven by a father who often searched for answers in all the wrong places. Through it all, they both love Jesus and as "Amazing Grace" declares, "Tis grace has brought [them] safe thus far." That is what this book is all about, the amazing grace of God.

This book is also evidence of the love and graciousness that is continuously demonstrated by the congregation, elders, and pastoral staff of Redemption Hills Church in Littleton, Colorado. Our dynamic church loves Jesus and is led by a senior pastor who is not a mascot of past piety but a redeemed sinner who transparently preaches and teaches the Word of God and cares for his flock in the best way he knows how.

They never begrudge me the time I need for solitude, prayer, writing, and fellowship. I am immensely blessed to minister with Pastor Blake Burget and Pastor Bruce Nickoley, and their wives Kristen and Marty, among other leaders and volunteers within our church, and I cherish the joy of living in fellowship with everybody at Redemption Hills Church.

It's a blessing that God has brought us together in such as way. I love you all!

INTRODUCTION

"Stu. It's Peter Ehrlichman. Are you free to talk?"

I broke into a cold sweat, not sure if I wanted to hear what my attorney was about to say. *I could use a drink right now!*

"Sure, Peter. What's up?"

"I'm with Kurt Hineline. Are you able to listen closely?"

"Just getting some things done in the warehouse. Go ahead."

"We wanted to let you know that the SEC decided to sue you on accounting fraud."

My head started spinning like a tornado, so I leaned against a stack of pallets to regain my balance. Surrounded by Chardonnays and Merlots, all I wanted was a vodka on the rocks.

"Stu? Are you there?"

"Yeah, I'm here."

"Not trying to add insult to injury, but on Monday the *Seattle Times* is going to run a story about you. It isn't going to be good."

Great! I thought. I'll be broke and unemployable when I get out. My life is over.

"Kurt and I are driving down to Portland to be with you. You're gonna be okay."

"No, you don't have to do that. I'm fine. Really." I lied. "Please, Peter and Kurt. Don't come. If you do, I won't meet with you. Wild horses couldn't drag me away to meet with you. I just need to be alone, so I can sort things out."

"If you insist," Peter replied. "But please let us know how we can help."

"Will do. We'll talk soon. Goodbye."

My life was coming to an end, which was good, because I needed a new one.

The minute I hung up my phone, I started calculating the closest distance to a drink. The town house that my wine distribution business rented for my business partner and me wasn't too far away, so I grabbed my keys, hopped into my gray BMW 750iL and headed to my escape.

Even if Peter and Kurt had driven down from Seattle, I wasn't planning on being at the town house when they arrived.

I knew it was time to make an exit.

Pulling into the parking space of my Nob Hill unit, I locked the car and practically ran up the stairs from the garage, through the front door, and straight to the kitchen. At this point, I had no shame. I just needed to escape. I threw my suit jacket over the island barstool, so I could get down to business and reached for some vodka from the cabinet above the sink in the kitchen.

That's when my phone rang. Considering my condition and not recognizing the phone number, I normally wouldn't have taken the call. For all I knew, it could have been a newspaper reporter, but for some reason I answered it.

"Hello?"

"Is this Stu Fuhlendorf?"

"Yeah, it is." I was in a bad mood and not at all interested in talking with anybody. "Who's this?"

"Stu, this is Chuck Colson."

I knew who Chuck Colson was—Richard Nixon's hatchet man during Watergate. He knew Peter Ehrlichman's father, John Ehrlichman, another Watergate alumnus. Chuck wrote about the experience and his Christian conversion in his book *Born Again*, which I had read a few years back.

There was no way I could be talking to Chuck Colson.

"Really?!" I snorted. "Pull this leg and it'll play 'Jingle Bells.' "

The voice on the other line chuckled.

"No, no. This is Chuck Colson."

"Really?" I then recognized his distinctive voice.

Guilty but Not Guilty

I thought about the things I had done in my life. I pridefully had pushed the envelope a number of times, and people could sue me and probably win. However, the charges the SEC was accusing me of—accounting fraud—I hadn't actually done. How ironic.

Little did I know that this crisis would lead me into a deeper understanding of Jesus Christ and the sovereign power of God. And, as it turned out, God would use it to bring some of his greatest blessings into my life.

In one sense, that day was the culmination of a dark period. It was the old story of the hotshot middle-aged fat-cat business executive who arrogantly builds his personal empire only to have it go down in flames. Between the ages of thirty and forty-four, I had taken three companies public, but at a price. When my world started to unravel, I was a three-hundred-plus-pound alcoholic.

But it's also the story of the great redemptive work of Jesus Christ in the life of somebody wholly unworthy of God's mercy and grace. It's a story of the truth and hope of the good news of Jesus Christ and his power to rescue the most despicable wretch.

If you're a business person, or anybody searching for true meaning, you'll learn how a good God can work all things together for his purpose through the mistakes and adversities in the life of a sinner.

While you will read about joyful times and raw, painful moments of my life, these are simply events pointing to a greater good. My point for writing this book is to demonstrate how an extravagantly merciful and gracious God can save an underserving, rebellious idolater from the miry depths of pride and rebellion. My great hope is that God will be glorified by this book and that you will be blessed and encouraged by the story of the amazing grace of Jesus Christ.

To God be the glory forever and ever. Amen.

ONE

SELF-SUFFICIENCY

My education in self-sufficiency began at an early age.

I was born in 1962 in Akron, Colorado, a small town of about one thousand people on the northeastern plains of the state. Like many rural communities, Akron has struggled to stem the steady migration of its young people into the city.

Today, a smaller number of vibrant ranchers and farmers comprise the community, and in many ways, it is a shell of a prior existence from the previous century. At times it looks like a ghost town in desperate pursuit of days long past. Adding insult to injury, the town hospital where I was born now functions as a nursing home, a sad harbinger of its future.

The roots of self-sufficiency run deep in my family. Both sides of the family were pioneers who settled in northeastern Colorado in the late 1880s. My Grandma Fuhlendorf grew up in a dirt-floored farmhouse in the country, northeast of Yuma, Colorado and didn't enjoy

7

the luxury of wood floors until she was a young adult. A product of the old west, self-reliant mentality, Grandma Fuhlendorf served as the matriarch of the family. She worked as a rural mail carrier for fifty-five years in Northeastern Colorado, famously delivering the mail in many generations of Volkswagen Bugs over the years. She passed her love of Volkswagen Bugs to me.

In addition to Grandma's mail carrier job, the Fuhlendorf family also managed the Yuma bowling alley and owned a hamburger joint and snack bar.

My great-grandparents on my mother's side, George and Zeporrah Brown, lived into their nineties and passed away in the mid-1970s. One of my great pleasures growing up was spending time listening to them tell stories of pioneering their way in the wild, wild west as youngsters. They waxed eloquently about their many adventures, joys, and hardships.

My mother's parents, Richard and Twila Ireland, whom I adoringly called Grampy and Grammy, worked the ranch and farm and lived nine miles away in Otis, Colorado, in the same house with my great-grandpa and grandma Brown. Their daughter and my mom, Lynn Ireland, was born in the farmhouse on that ranch.

Mom and Dad were high school sweethearts and married right after they graduated from Yuma High School. Mom was eighteen and dad was nineteen. A year later, she gave birth to me. That's how it was done in those days, especially in rural communities. Graduate from high school. Then get married, go to work, and start a family.

My dad, Elvin, spent most of his career as an employee with Home, Light and Power and then Public Service Company, both utilities companies. Dad was a disciplinarian and unafraid to take the belt to me when I misbehaved. Like his generational predecessors, he believed in discipline and proper roles.

My mother spent the early part of their marriage as a homemaker, and later, out of necessity, worked as a payroll clerk and a secretary. She modeled a work ethic that was relentlessly energetic from sunup to sundown until the day she died.

I Came by My Work Ethic Naturally

From the time I was seven or eight years old, I happily spent every summer and winter break at Grampy and Grammy's ranch and farm. The rest of the year, I lived in Greeley with my parents, who had moved there so Dad could support his family.

Grampy and Grammy's house sat directly across from Doll-up Bu-Tee Bar, which was a hair stylist salon shop owned by the Haverland family. Old stage coach wagon wheels embellished the perimeter, complemented by lilac bushes and flowers. The main floor included three bedrooms that accommodated my great-grandparents, Grampy and Grammy, and any guest who might stay overnight.

Grammy and her neighbor to the west, Phyllis Amick, nurtured a large garden a block down the alley from both homes, and together they generated enough vegetables to last an entire year for both families. There was a chicken coup next to the garden with enough chickens to provide ample poultry for meals. Many days we would whack off the head of a chicken, hang it upside down on the clothes line, then dress and pluck the dead bird for supper.

In a close-knit community like Otis, neighbors didn't knock on the door. They walked right in, sat down in the living room, and struck up a conversation. Politics and business were always welcome topics and formality was nonexistent.

The Amicks's property also included a junkyard. On July 4, 1971, my cousin Devin Nelson and I were secretly playing with fireworks in the side alley and accidently set the Amick grass and garage on fire. The townspeople quickly put out the flames with minimal damage. Grampy gave us a good talking to, and my dad took a belt to my backside because of our thoughtless and rebellious behavior.

Grammy worked at the Bu-Tee Bar as a hair stylist from time to time to bring in extra income. Grampy woke up every morning before dawn to eat breakfast and head out to work until sundown.

When Devin and I spent the night at their house, Grampy put me in charge of changing the end gun on the sprinklers at two in the morning to keep them from watering the county roads. Then, we'd get up early the next morning and work until the sun went down.

While the ranch and farm weren't particularly big, the soil was perfect for growing corn and wheat, and there was grazing land to feed the cattle. My grandparents owned about 150 head of cattle, plus dry and irrigated farmland. While toiling all day in the unrelenting sun of northeastern Colorado may not seem like fun to people accustomed to playing video games and working in air-conditioned surroundings, I absolutely loved it and still hold many fond memories.

Devin and I enjoyed numerous summers on the ranch and farm, learning by day what it means to work hard, be responsible, and grow up. Picking yourself up by your bootstraps wasn't a badge of honor in our family and community, it was a way of life.

Early on, my cousin proved he was a better farmer and rancher than me. A long day in the fields often sent me to bed with eyes nearly swollen shut from my hay fever. Grammy would then give me raw potatoes to place on my bloated eyes.

When I was ten, Grampy said to me, "Since you're not going to be a farmer, you're coming with me, so you can see what a banker does." Many times he hauled me off to the Yuma or Otis bank to sit in a business meeting with one of the local bankers.

Grampy and Grammy were anchors in my life when my immediate family became unhinged. When he wasn't working around the ranch, Grampy was absolutely one of the great joys in my life. A little Irishman with a huge sense of humor, duty, and an old-fashioned Puritan work ethic, he used to tell me, "Stu, there are no shortcuts; quit complaining and get tough with it."

Not only was Grampy a hard-working farmer and rancher, he also was a veteran of World War II. He served his country in the Pacific Theatre on the USS *Rowan*. No matter how menial the job, every task was equally important, and he always told the truth, which I tried to do as well.

But it wasn't all work and no play during the summers of my youth in Otis. For two years in elementary school, my cousin Devin and I played on a T-ball team that Olinger Mortuary sponsored. Grammy was our manager and coach. I played first base, Devin played second, Donny Anderson played shortstop, and Mark Anderson played third. The Kjildegaard boys manned the outfield.

My grandmother expertly led us to two undefeated seasons and two T-ball championships. Both trophies were displayed proudly in the mortuary lobby. Her coaching attire was unconventional for a successful manager: pink polyester Bermuda stretch shorts and a white blouse. But her instruction was mysteriously wise in the great American pastime.

When Devin and I were eight years old, Grampy and Grammy offered us a deal we couldn't refuse.

"We have $100 that we'd like to give to both of you," they said. "And you get to choose one of two things to do with it: we'll either buy you a calf, which you have to promise to raise and eventually sell, or we'll get you a musical instrument like a piano, which you have to promise to learn to play."

Devin opted for the cow and I picked the piano. Little did we know this investment would pay dividends later in our lives.

Grammy was a piano teacher and she instilled in me a lifelong love of music. She gave me piano lessons when I was younger, and then for many years I studied with other teachers and honed my musical skills on my own.

By the eighth grade I was playing keyboard in a rock and roll band called Self-Employed (derived from Bachman Turner Overdrive's song "Taking Care of Business"). We excelled to the point that we started playing gigs in the area—junior and senior high dances, Elks Club pool parties, and places like that. I actually made enough money to pay some of my bills and sustain myself while my parents were going through their difficulties. Devin ended up competing as a bull rider.

The Devastation

From the outward appearance, we seemed like the all-American family and my parents seemed to enjoy a healthy marriage. Alas, rarely is there ever such a thing. After about sixteen years, for a variety of reasons, including both infidelity and growing apart, they divorced.

I was fourteen years old.

They tried to reconcile a few times, but the pain of the sin and betrayal were too much to overcome. My mother was heartbroken, and I imagine my father felt much the same—yet he seemed unable to push away from his secret life and longing for the other woman.

That period was profoundly painful for the entire family, especially my mom.

Their last attempt to reconcile in 1976 did not go well. To numb the pain, mom washed down some tranquilizers with a bottle of wine and was unmistakably drunk. My parents started to fight, and my dad announced he was moving out.

Knowing that the rage couldn't continue, I defended him. I just couldn't take it anymore. Mom grabbed a knife and threatened to kill my dad. She was overcome by the lingering suffering of a broken marriage and told him, "I'm sick of the pain and want this to end!" I held her knife-laden hand in the air as my dad packed his bags and left the family for the last time. As he drove off, my mother dropped to the floor and broke down in tears. Then I wrapped my arm around her as we both sobbed.

Life moved on, and we never discussed it again. My mom married five more times before meeting Larry Pickrell, whom she loved dearly and with whom she spent the last twenty-eight years of her life.

Unless you've experienced it firsthand, most people can't comprehend the devastation caused by divorce. I tried to escape the pain of watching my family disintegrate by spending my extra time with friends and their families. I also relied on athletics, music and my own self-determination.

And then there was Grampy and Grammy. Like me, they were heartbroken by my parents' divorce and welcomed me into their home during my summers and Christmas break. More than anyone, Grampy and Grammy modeled love and the importance of buckling down and moving forward. I learned to shut down my emotions and work harder. Initially, that became my drug of choice.

Self-sufficiency.

My Religion? Me!

Ironically, during this time, my grandparents began looking for answers to some of life's ultimate questions and dabbled in the Jehovah's Witnesses. We attended Kingdom Hall meetings together and delivered *Watchtower* magazines door-to-door. Although Grampy was a World War II vet, we'd turn our backs to the flag during tractor pulls and rodeos. We also didn't celebrate birthdays or Christmas in my grandparents' house.

I found all of this confusing; the contradictions I saw between Jehovah's Witnesses and other religions and cults led me to believe that religion was a crutch for the needy and broken. Ironically, that belief holds true for every follower of Jesus Christ. Our faith is available only to the needy and broken.

When I was younger, my parents attended the First Christian Church in Greeley. They brought my sisters and me every week, and we did our best to involve ourselves. One week, I even delivered a youth sermon to the congregation for Youth Sunday. My dad was an usher, and my mom was involved in women's Bible study groups.

But when my family suffered through the many issues associated with divorce, various people in the church acted unnecessarily strict and judgmental toward us, basically shunning us. My mom particularly felt like the church turned their back on her when she needed them most.

I decided they were a bunch of hypocrites and blamed God for their behavior. "How could a loving God allow people to act like that? How could people go to church for years and act differently than Jesus said we should act?" I asked myself. There seemed to be no fruit from many of the people who called themselves Christians. So after the divorce, my mom no longer wasted her time with church—and I no longer wasted my time with God. We never returned, in fact, and in our home, religion ceased to exist.

Our aversion to the church fueled my obsession with becoming self-sufficient. I didn't need God. Depending upon anyone or anything but myself was weakness. Over time, I grew hostile toward the thought of God's existence. I couldn't rely on my parents. I couldn't rely on God. The only person I could rely on was me.

Sports Became My Escape

In previous generations, farmers didn't put much stock in education, and my family was no different. Grampy worked hard all the way through high school and then after earning his diploma, he directed all of his energies to working the family ranch and farm. Life was too busy to waste time on further education. But not for me. I wanted to be the first person in my family to graduate from college, even if I had to put myself through school. To this day, I'm still the only person from my immediate family to graduate from college.

My sophomore year, I enrolled at University High School, a private school at the University of Northern Colorado in Greeley. I worked hard on my studies and eventually landed on the honor roll. While I was a decent student, sports became my escape. I spent hours and hours in the high school and college gyms playing basketball, doing anything to avoid being at home. I loved my mom and sisters to death but going home meant entering into their stress and pain.

During that time, I devised the perfect rotation to avoid our family mess: football in the fall, basketball in the winter, and track and field in the spring. Then during the summers, I lived with Grampy and Grammy. If I had any spare time, I played more gigs with my band or I hung out with my friends and their families who took me under their wing. All my friends lived with both parents, most were educated, white collar. Some were very well off. My friends' parents stoked my desire for advanced education and success.

Basketball became my primary obsession. I hoped to attract enough attention to earn a scholarship to pay for college. Growing up in a poor, broken family, that was the only logical way to fund my schooling.

My junior year, I was named to the all-conference team as a guard which only fed my burgeoning ego. Looking at the crowds who came to see our team play, I couldn't resist letting the attention go to my head. "They're coming to see *me!*" I thought.

Intoxicated by the adulation, I began challenging my coaches. Once, during a game, I argued with the coach, who immediately pulled me out of the game. During the time out, the head coach walked over to me as I sulked at the end of the bench.

"What's wrong with you?" he asked.

I couldn't believe that he would pull me out of the game; I was so much better than everybody else.

Who Needs Anyone?

Self-sufficiency. I knew better than anyone else, and I didn't need anyone else.

By the time my senior year rolled around, I began receiving recruiting letters. Division I schools paid very little attention to me, but a few Division II schools and NAIA colleges showed interest. This only stoked the fires of my pride and quest for autonomy. Soon I could move away from the brokenness of my family and fend for myself.

My senior year, we were one of the highest ranked teams in the state and drew big crowds at every game. As the season progressed, we won the districts and regionals, and I was named to the all-state team.

We breezed through the state quarterfinals. In the semifinals we faced Lewis Palmer High School, the number-one team in the state. We were ranked second, so it was going to be a showdown. In the last few minutes of the game, we were ahead by six points, forcing Lewis Palmer to foul us.

Standing at the free throw line in the fourth quarter, I presumed all the work and effort I had put into basketball was going to pay off. I was the leading scorer in our league, and one of the top scorers in the state of Colorado, so surely I was up to the task of finishing this game off. But in the last quarter, I missed five crucial free throws, and we lost the game 66-64. I never felt more devastated in my life. For hours, I huddled in the locker room and wept. Self-sufficiency hadn't led to perfection; it only led to pressure-filled performance—and failure for myself and my teammates.

Despite the devastating loss, multiple schools recruited me, and I ultimately accepted a scholarship to Doane College, a small NAIA school 475 miles away in Crete, Nebraska. Doane College also awarded me a music scholarship to sing, compose music, and play piano. So,

I was going to college as both a musician and a jock. I looked forward to finishing my final semester at University High School.

By the end of my senior year, I had convinced myself that I could achieve anything I set my mind to do. Honor role? Check! Musician in a rock and roll band? Check! All-state basketball player? Check! Scholarship to pay for college? Check!

My parents were very happy that I would be going to college on a scholarship. But not as happy as me. That was the payoff for all the hard work. Self-sufficiency.

On a sun-filled summer day in late August of 1980 I loaded up my VW bug and my friend Kevin loaded up his Datsun pickup truck and off to college we went to room together.

Six and a half hours later I pulled into the school parking lot. Up to that point, I was cocky but still a pretty straight kid. As I walked onto the campus and into the gym, I said to myself, "This is for me. This is where my hard work and my self-sufficiency is paying off."

My life at the young age of eighteen seemed to be on the right track. Little did I know that my growing self-sufficiency would take a left turn, and I would start doing things in college that would carry ramifications for the rest of my life.

TWO

FIRST LOVE

"**K**evin, dude, I'm stoked. Isn't this awesome? I can't wait to hit the court and meet the girls around here."

"It feels good to be on our own, doesn't it?" Kevin said as he nodded his head.

We were both a little out of breath carrying our personal items into our dorm room at Smith Hall. After transporting our stuff, we smirked at each other, ready to start our new adventure.

Although at fifty thousand people Greeley, Colorado was ten times the size of Crete, Nebraska, I felt relieved to escape the stress of home and start over again in new surroundings—rural southeastern Nebraska! I was ready to be the big fish in a small pond. And the ninety-six-degree temperature and 96 percent humidity on that late August afternoon didn't faze me. Besides, it was my birthday!

After emptying my VW Bug, I headed over to the gym, where I worked out, shot some hoops, and met with my new college basketball coach, Bob Erickson.

Since basketball season didn't start until October, I decided to try out for the golf team and the school chorale and made both. I was excited to play golf competitively and introduce some music into my new surroundings. Anything to bide my time until the basketball season started. Who needs academics?

Peppermint Schnapps

Homecoming week mid-October 1980 marked a turning point in my life. "Dollar" Bill Anderson lived on the same floor as me. His magnetic personality and wicked sense of humor made him the life of our floor. We decided to throw a party on a Friday night, and I eventually ended up sitting on a recliner in his room. Dollar Bill's room and our floor was filled with laughing, partying college students. I'm sure the scene was replicated on college campuses across the country that night.

Up to that point, my lips had never touched alcohol. As a dedicated athlete, I didn't want to ingest anything that would harm my body or jeopardize my eligibility. Until that night.

"Hey Stu, you want a shot of this?" Dollar Bill asked me, as he held a bottle in his hand.

"What is it?"

"Peppermint schnapps. You'll love it!"

"Sure, why not?"

I held the bottle to my lips, not sure what to expect. The sweet, minty smell rushed up my nose, clearing everything in its path. Then this rookie took a swig and everything changed.

Liquid euphoria!

I imbibed three or four more shots before wobbling my way off his recliner.

A surge of exhilaration coursed through my veins as I exited the room and entered the hallway. The pressures of school, the stress of my home life, all the negative emotions I worked so hard to suppress were suddenly gone. I was free!

Up and down the hallway I ran, arms in the air, yelling "Woo-hoo!" I was darting around students, spilling their drinks. I didn't care.

Finally, some basketball players and other students caught me and escorted me back to Dollar Bill's room.

"Somebody take him back," I vaguely remember a voice saying.

It was my first—and certainly not my last—drinking experience.

Nobody Else Could See It but Me

Basketball season couldn't begin soon enough, but it eventually arrived. I couldn't wait to showcase my skills to Coach Erickson and the female students at Doane College. But much to my surprise, our team was stocked with great players, even though we were playing at the NAIA level. I realized that many of my teammates were all-state players in high school, just like me. Nevertheless, I was confident that I would fit in, make the varsity team, and hopefully get quite a bit of playing time my freshman year.

As the basketball season grew near, it became clear to me that I was going to spend more time on the bench than on the court, which for most freshmen would be fine. But for someone as proud as me, it didn't sit well.

Basketball practices became increasingly difficult for me. I felt like I was putting in a great effort with little return. I soon became quite dissatisfied. My pride blinded me to the many good players on our team. In my eighteen-year-old mind, I just couldn't understand why my coaches weren't aware of my superior basketball talent.

As the season began, I determined that I wasn't going to suffer the humiliation of sitting on the bench more than I should. If my coaches weren't going to recognize my abilities, I'd take my talents to another coach at another school.

And I tried.

Without Coach Erickson's knowledge, I called Tony McAndrews, the coach at Colorado State University, a Division 1 school. We knew each other from my high school days. After I explained to him that I was interested in transferring, he told me he didn't have any scholarships available and suggested I remain at Doane.

He obviously didn't get it.

Over Christmas break, I explained my predicament to my father.

"Dad," I began. "I want to look at other colleges."

"Son," he said, "I got married when I was nineteen years old. I attended college for a year and a half. Then I dropped out of college my second year and never went back. It was one of the worst decisions of my life. I'm frightened that you'll do the same. It's a terrible decision to quit. I want you to go back to school in Nebraska, and I don't care whether you play ball or not. Go back!"

I took his advice—at least temporarily—and stayed at Doane. But three weeks into the season, I dropped off the basketball team and looked to transfer to a school in Colorado. I was much too proud to explain to my dad that I was homesick, and that I missed my high school girlfriend. My immaturity was derailing the opportunity to transition into adulthood. Rather than learn the importance of perseverance, I opted for the easy way out. Entitlement was as intoxicating as that first drink of Peppermint Schnapps.

Before summer break, I called Thurm Wright, the basketball coach at the University of Northern Colorado (UNC) in Greeley, a Division 2 school. Coach Wright knew me from high school and the university was in my hometown.

"Stu," Coach Wright told me. "I don't have a scholarship for you, but you're welcome to try out for the team. If you make it, you can walk on and possibly earn a basketball scholarship."

That's all I needed to hear.

So after one year at Doane College, I packed my Volkswagen Bug and drove back to my hometown of Greeley, Colorado. In the fall of 1981, I enrolled at UNC. The NCAA rules stipulated that transfers were required to sit out a year, so I sharpened my basketball skills, focused on academics, and indulged my newfound love for alcohol. Every weekend I partied at Orville's Hangar or the Armory, drinking as much as I could handle. Back then, beers with 3.2 percent alcohol by weight was legal for anyone eighteen or older—and plenty of beer joints in town gladly accommodated us.

Entering my third year of college, UNC made a change and Ron Brillhart was named the new coach. Coach Brillhart didn't know me, but I had to try out for the team again. This didn't go well for my ego. I made the team, but once again I found that I would be sitting at the far end of the bench, honing my skills more as team encourager than player. That was enough college basketball for me. Another clueless coach who didn't get it. My ego couldn't take it any longer, so once and for all, I quit playing college basketball.

My drinking continued to increase, and many mornings I woke up with a hangover—and at times next to a woman whose name I didn't even know. This became part of my lifestyle, though I was able to get through classes and work towards a teaching degree.

My nights of heavy drinking and partying made getting up for class nearly impossible, turning me into an average student. I didn't have the capacity to drink just a beer or two early in the evening. Drinking dominated my activities well into the night.

During that time, I grew increasingly antagonistic to the Christian faith. Authors like Bertrand Russell and Christopher Hitchens informed my postmodern view of self-made morality and validated my burgeoning agnosticism and growing opinion that God didn't exist. It was the perfect "faith" for a person who didn't want to be dependent upon anyone else.

A Stiff Cocktail

Late summer 1985, after graduating from UNC with a degree in social science education, I moved to Denver to substitute teach while looking for a full-time teaching position. Just as classes started, I helped my good friend Kevin move to New York City to attend New York University. While there, I stopped by the office of a French company named Club Med and applied for a job. A month later they offered me a job at their Copper Mountain resort, where I would work in the bar and help run the nightclub.

Two weeks later I began a six-month stint that could only be described as a cocktail of narcissism and hedonism. A little bit like Sodom and Gomorrah. I lived on-site, and during happy hour I played the piano and sang for the guests with a cocaine addict named Doug. At 6:30 I bartended in the lobby bar and then at 9:00 p.m. I moved to the nightclub until we shut everything down at 2:00 in the morning.

My nights overflowed with vodka and cranberry juice cocktails and even some cocaine. Countless evenings I drank too much, danced with the guests, and at times spent the night with a young woman I hooked up with in the night club. Then I woke up the next morning and skied until mid-afternoon before soaking in a hot tub, enjoying a drink or two, and starting the process all over again with Doug at happy hour. This took place six days a week.

Though I enjoyed aspects of the hedonistic lifestyle, by the end of the ski season, I was ready to move on with my life. The excesses were weighing on my conscience, though I didn't know why. I knew the lifestyle was unhealthy and could possibly suck me into a vortex from which I could never escape. I was also starting to date a former cheerleader from Auburn University named Tina.

My dad didn't help things.

"Are you crazy?" he said to me when I asked him for advice. "Why wouldn't you stay at Club Med?"

Nevertheless, I decided to move to look for a teaching job. In May 1986, Tina helped me move in with my dad in Denver. But when she met my family and the poverty and chaos we lived in, she ended the relationship. So I went from partying every night, women, and hot tubs to living with my father, sleeping on the couch, and looking for a new job.

I quickly received an assignment to teach at Denver East High School, which lasted until the end of the school year. At night I worked as a bartender at Lone Tree Country Club. I loved it because I could play the piano with Robert Blakey, the grandson of Art Blakey, a legendary jazz drummer. Perks of working at the country club included free drinks and free golf. My days consisted of teaching history and social studies, and my afternoons were all about free drinks and golf.

And Then Came Trish

A few weeks into my new life, my friend Kevin and I decided to spend the evening at Basins Up, a club in downtown Denver. A great local rhythm and blues band—The Freddi-Henchi Band—was performing, so we both downed a pint of Jack Daniels at his place and left. Kevin and I were enjoying some beverages at the club when a friend he knew from Colorado State University showed up.

"Stu," Kevin began. "I'd like you to meet Mary. We went to Colorado State together. Mary is a Tri-Delt."

Not long into the conversation, another woman approached.

"Hi, Mary, who are your friends?" the woman asked with a grin on her face.

Mary introduced Trish to Kevin and Kevin introduced Trish to me.

"Trish, meet my friend Stu," Kevin said but just couldn't leave it at that. "He's a professional surfer from Newport Beach, California."

Trish's good looks left me dumbfounded. I was immediately enthralled, but her countenance changed upon hearing Kevin's lie. So I decided to get her on the dance floor and away from Kevin ASAP.

I found out much later that Trish had eyed me from across the bar. I was wearing very short Ocean Pacific corduroy shorts (back when they were cool. *Really!*). It was early May and still cold outside, so I'm pretty sure I was the only one in the bar wearing summer attire. But Trish noticed. When she saw her friend Mary talking to Kevin, that was her in.

We stepped out on the dance floor, and within one or two dances, she asked me about living in California. Little did I know that Trish had spent time in Newport Beach, so I found myself descending deeper and deeper into Kevin's lie. I discovered that Trish was a twenty-three-year-old engineer who worked at Martin Marietta in Denver. Everything about her mesmerized me.

I knew I wanted to get to know this woman better. "Trish" I finally confessed, "I'm not really a professional surfer. I'm a schoolteacher at Denver East High School, and I work on the side as a bartender in Lone Tree."

Not only did a look of relief flood over her, but she informed me, "Denver East is my alma mater!" We were clicking.

By the fourth or fifth dance, we started slow dancing, even though the music was going fast. The world disappeared except for the two of us.

We spent the rest of the evening dancing, talking, and getting to know each other. At one point I stepped away and proclaimed to some old friends who had joined us, "I'm going to marry that woman!" They chuckled and then I went back to Trish and continued our evening.

When it was time to leave, I asked Trish if she would drive me home. Kevin drove us to the club, so I really *did* need a ride. She said she would be happy to.

"Trish, do you want to come inside?" I asked her during the drive. Obviously, I had ulterior motives.

"Um, I don't think that'll work tonight."

"Oh, c'mon. We can have a nightcap, and you can be on your way."

"Absolutely not!" she laughed. "I know men like you!"

Then she dropped me off at Kevin's apartment complex.

I tried my best to sleep with her that night, but she handled me in a very mature way. Although I failed at seducing her, I did succeed at convincing her to give me her phone number.

The next morning, I asked myself, "Is this somebody who's worth calling on the phone?"

I picked up the phone and dialed her.

"Hello?" she answered.

"Trish, this is Stu Fuhlendorf. You may remember me."

She laughed, and we were on our way.

We decided to meet for coffee, and I offered to pick her up at her apartment in Littleton—on my Yamaha 850 Special. I had gotten rid of my VW. I didn't mind because that meant she would hold on to me while we rode off into the sunset.

When she answered the door, she looked even more beautiful than the previous evening. We went out for coffee, and I learned later that the exhaust pipe on my motorcycle burned her calf. Trish eventually told me that she thought, "This better work out because I've been branded!" From that time forward, we spent every spare moment together.

Trish Fuhlendorf

Three months into our budding romance, Trish and I drove to Copper Mountain and rode the ski lift to the top. It was late summer.

"So, how long have we been dating?" I asked.

"Three months," Trish answered.

"So, when are we going to get married?" I asked, trying to remain calm. I was completely caught up in the moment and not prepared with a ring. Not to mention, I wasn't sure how I could even afford one.

"Is that your way of asking me to get married?" she asked incredulously. "You're assuming the sale!"

"Yes, I suppose I am." I smiled.

"I accept," she laughed and then gave me a kiss.

As we planned our wedding, I learned that Trish grew up in a Roman Catholic family. Her dad was a Double-Domer, meaning he earned his undergraduate and graduate law degree from Notre Dame. (He had passed away from cancer a few years before.) Trish attended Catholic schools before attending Denver East High School. But at the time, she wasn't a practicing Catholic or a Christian.

To honor her mom, though, we agreed to hold a Catholic wedding, which meant enrolling in and attending the Roman Catholic Engaged Encounter retreat. It was uncomfortable, as we were living together, and the truth came out in the paperwork we filled out. Oh well.

We got married in Trish's mom's church, St. Vincent De Paul. In all, 250 people attended. Since I wasn't a Christian, I didn't care if we married in a Buddhist temple or Circus Circus chapel in Vegas. I just wanted to marry her.

Afterwards, a family friend provided us with a chauffeur-driven Rolls Royce, and we drove to our reception at Cherry Hills Country Club. The highlight was drinking champagne from Trish's shoe! We snuck away from the reception later that evening and spent our wedding night at the Westin Hotel in downtown Denver. The next day we flew to Hawaii for a ten-day honeymoon.

Only eleven months after we met, we were now husband and wife. We were still getting to know each other, but love overcame many of the obstacles and difficulties of a young marriage.

Then I Met a New Love

Just before the wedding, the father of a friend started a mutual fund company and offered me a job selling securities. I knew very little about business because I had a teaching degree, but Ed Pittock was willing to mentor me. Ed founded the stockbrokerage firm E. J. Pittock and Company right out of my alma mater, the University of Northern Colorado, where he was also an all-American quarterback. His mutual fund company, Continental Heritage, was his new venture.

I immediately loved the job, but I particularly liked analyzing and assessing companies. I found myself spending more time with the portfolio manager, Doug Helm, learning how to analyze the strategy and financial performance of companies, than selling the funds—which was my paid position.

Convinced that I had found my niche, I began exploring business schools, so I could earn my MBA. Trish was a human factors aerospace engineer at the time, and was ready to move on, so she applied at a few different aerospace companies—one in Maryland, one in Nashville, and one in San Diego. General Dynamics in San Diego offered her a job. So in 1987 we decided to move there, and I was accepted and enrolled in the MBA program at the University of San Diego.

We fell in love with San Diego and spent many evenings drinking and playing shuffleboard at different bars and nightclubs around the city with newfound friends. San Diego was a perfect fit for us at that time in our lives. Trish worked and supported us while I worked full-time on my MBA, which I absolutely loved.

After I graduated from business school in 1989, Trish and I applied for jobs at Martin Marietta back in Denver. Martin offered her an engineering job designing a robotic arm for a space station, and they offered me a job in financial program management. So, we moved back to Colorado to start our new life, which included starting a family with the birth of my son, Erich, in 1990.

After a year and a half, I moved into the corporate development side of the aerospace business and started feeling less and less satisfied working for a mega-company. I wanted to work for a smaller business and strengthen my business leadership skills. I preferred being a big fish in a small pond.

During that time, an executive commented to me, "Stu, I just want you to know that you're highly thought of in the company. We'd like to move you into a different role with our business development group. Additionally, some cost cuts are coming, and this would help protect your job."

"Thanks," I replied. "Let me think about it."

At that moment, the same sense of superiority that afflicted me during my basketball days struck again.

"You know, I am pretty gifted," I thought. "I've always outperformed my coworkers, and they're finally seeing it. They may be more educated than me or come from wealthier families, but they can't outperform me."

Self-sufficiency.

Pride.

While working at Martin Marietta was a good gig, I wasn't sure I wanted to stay. I could take the new job or let them cut me. But in the end, I wanted to build a business and be a leader on my own terms.

After talking to Trish, I went back to Martin Marietta and said, "I appreciate the offer; I know that you're doing some cost-cutting as well. I'd just as soon leave and find a job with a smaller company and move into leadership where I can use my skills to help the business grow."

So, in 1991, with a one-year-old little boy, I resigned my job at Martin Marietta. I didn't know what I was going to do next, but I knew I wanted to be in control in a business leadership position. I felt like I could do it better than anyone I had worked with. I was full of pride, self-sufficiency, and my first love—me.

THREE

CHASING THE GOLD

In 1991, Colorado voters legalized gambling in three Colorado towns: Cripple Creek (near Colorado Springs), Blackhawk, and Central City (the latter two near Denver).

About that time, I sat on the back deck of my home one evening, drinking beers and Jack Daniels with my good friend and Martin Marietta colleague Mark Heffner.

"Heeefff!" I implored my good friend. "I can smell the money coming out of the Rocky Mountains. The scent of green is strong, and it ain't the pine trees."

"Dooorff!" he chimed back. "If anybody would risk mining poker chips out of the mountains, you'd be the one."

I sat there smiling at him with a beer in one hand, a shot of whiskey in the other, as visions of becoming a tycoon in the Colorado gambling industry danced in my head.

There was "gold in them thar hills." I decided to pour all my energies into learning everything I could about the gambling industry. I couldn't have cared less about the ethics or morals of gambling; I just knew there was money to be made. So I enrolled in a blackjack and poker dealing class in a strip mall to learn the ins and outs—dealing from the shoe, counting the drop, spotting the shills, and so forth—of legalized gambling.

I focused my sights on breaking into the legalized gaming industry. I applied for a key gaming license, which involved a background check administered by the FBI under the supervision of the Colorado Gaming License Office. The license allowed me to work as an employee and owner in the gambling industry.

After I passed the background check, I put out my feelers throughout Colorado through an industry expert to see who was looking to invest and/or build casinos. I also started walking the streets of Blackhawk and Central City, looking for opportunities. Buildings were under construction or renovation as casinos were preparing to open to the public.

One day, as I made my way up Main Street in Black Hawk, I spotted a small old west saloon that was being renovated. The front door to the Rohling Inn Casino was ajar, so I stepped inside. A little man with a dome-wrap haircut and a cigarette in his hand was directing people setting up the casino.

"My name's Stu Fuhlendorf," I said as I stuck my hand in his direction.

The man ignored my invitation to shake hands and instead looked me up and down. I could tell I was wasting his time.

"OK, so you are." Then he turned his head to the side. "Johnny!" he yelled. "I need you to move those chairs to the front of the barroom."

"Mine's George," he said as he looked back at me. I could tell I was running out of time. "How can I help you?"

"I'd like to break into the gambling industry. I've gone to gaming school, worked in industry, and have applied for my gaming license."

"Yeah, why are you telling me that?" George asked.

"Because I'd like to help you build this casino," I said boldly without having a clue who I was talking to.

"We're looking to build a staff, but I haven't started interviewing yet."

"Well, I'd like to help you build the staff."

George chuckled.

"Just give me your resume, and if we need you, we'll call you."

I gave George my resume and every morning for the next three days, I paid a visit to the Rohling Inn, sat on the outside stairs, and said hi to my impatient friend. I pestered him about my qualifications and then continued my job search. Later, I found out that George Thompson was the new general manager of the casino. He had been recruited from Steve Wynn's Golden

Nugget in Las Vegas, where he worked as the head of slot operations.

On my fourth day, George and another gentleman passed me on the way down the stairs. "Stu, this is John Lester. He owns the Rohling Casino. He wants to talk to you."

John and I stepped into another room and discussed my job experience, my qualifications, and the finer details of the casino business. Little did I know that our conversation was a job interview. The next day, I made my perfunctory visit to the Rohling Inn. George and John again passed by my normal spot on the stairs.

"Stu," George began. "We'd like to talk to you about working as our controller."

Just like that I officially broke into the gaming industry, just weeks before the casino opened, and with much work ahead of me to build the team.

Dealing with Disillusionment

The weeks leading up to the opening were packed with staff interviews, setting up the accounting system, working with the state gaming regulators, and trying to keep up with hundreds of moving parts. The casino was embellished with a British flair—red velvet curtains and oil paintings of fox hunts.

With just a few hours before we unlocked the doors on opening day, long lines of people began forming outside. One patron in line looked straight out of the 1850s, down to the pearl-handled gun in his belt holster. Employees checked and rechecked the decor and tested the slot machines to ensure they were in working order.

Finally, the doors opened and people rushed in. Immediately, I asked our new patron to give me his gun until he was ready to leave. I returned it to him as he left in the early morning hours. For a while, I dealt blackjack at one of the tables.

Though the state of Colorado only allowed a five-dollar maximum on bets, gambling proved extremely lucrative to the many casinos, including the Rohling Inn. As time progressed, I learned more and more about the industry: how to keep the books, oversee security, monitor the monies that flowed in and out of the casino, and everyday operations.

But one facet really wore me down: watching older men and women come in, cash out their Social Security or pension checks, and then deposit all their money into the slot machines. Over and over I watched this sad ritual take place. I couldn't understand why these people with limited means were chasing the dream of a large jackpot when the odds were stacked against them. I also felt some angst about how willingly we collected their money without batting an eye.

As the casino flourished, I worked longer and longer hours trying to keep up with my responsibilities. My son, Erich, was beginning to walk, and my daughter Hannah was on the way. To my regret, I didn't spend as much time with them in the early years as I should have.

I worked late hours and then hung around the place to drink with my coworkers and play some poker. Obviously, the horrendous work hours began affecting my marriage to Trish.

Late one Friday night while I was working the casino, two beautiful female colleagues began flirting with me at one of the tables. Our back-and-forth culminated with a proposition from both women for a threesome later that night. These kinds of situations tend to find their way into the gambling industry.

My heart was racing, and my hormones began raging. Up till then I had only ever imagined such an opportunity. I stuck my left hand in my pocket to hide my wedding ring. I wasn't hiding it from them; they knew I was married. I didn't want my ring to get in the way of my decision.

"Well, I don't know," I answered. "I have plans this weekend and I need to be up early tomorrow."

"It's your choice," one of the women answered, reaching into her purse. "If you have a change of mind, just come pay us a visit tonight."

She wrote her address on a piece of paper and handed it to me.

"We'll be waiting for you," she said as she winked at me.

"It's a definite possibility," I responded, hoping the two lovely ladies couldn't see my wobbly knees. "Keep the light on for me."

My thoughts swirled around my head at a frantic pace later that night as I drove the long windy road out of Blackhawk. Trish was very pregnant with Hannah at that time, which didn't help. My long work hours paired with a lack of intimacy common during the final trimester made the decision that much more difficult.

"If I take those ladies up on their offer," I thought, "I can just tell Trish I worked late and decided to spend the night at the office. She'll never know.

"But she's my wife. What if Trish finds out? How could I do this to her?"

Driving home, I knew the road would eventually lead me to I-70. I could head east to the ladies' apartment and drive a wedge between me and my wife that would be nearly impossible to remove.

Or I could head west on I-70 and drive to Dillon where the family was staying that night in our mountain condo. Suppressing my hormones would save my marriage.

Would I sacrifice my future with Trish for an unforgettable night of fun and debauchery?

As I approached I-70, I knew the course of the rest of my life was at stake. The pressure mounted. I pulled the car to the side of the road to calm down and weigh the pros and cons of my decision. I loved my wife dearly, but I had a "live and let live" philosophy of life. My morality was based on *my* definition of right and wrong, so I had no qualms about committing adultery. I loved my wife and kids. Where the love came from, I'm not sure since I didn't believe in a loving deity.

I put the car into gear and slowly drove toward the fork in the road. I didn't know which direction I would go but suddenly found myself heading west toward Trish. The further down the road I drove, the stronger I felt.

"Yes," I said to myself. "This is the right decision. I'm making the right decision! I need to tell Trish that I chose her!"

When I arrived at our condo, I motioned at Trish to meet me alone in our bedroom. Then I shared with her the conversation earlier that evening.

"Trish, I faced a situation tonight that threw me for a loop that I think you should know about."

"What is it?" she said.

I told her about the proposal for a ménage à trois, and my decision to turn right instead of left.

"I don't want you doing this anymore," she said as our conversation came to an abrupt close.

Confessing my verdict to Trish felt like a burden was lifted off my shoulders, but that wasn't the case for her. While she felt relieved by my decision, the fact that I even considered the threesome crushed her. How could she compete with them?

Time to Dust Off My Rolodex

In the upcoming year, I became increasingly disenchanted with the "gaming" industry, partly because of how it affected Trish and partly due to the nature of the business. I concluded that it was barely a step above the strip club business. About that time, my mother informed me that a small, private electronics contract manufacturing company named Electronic Fab Technology Corp (EFTC) in Greeley, Colorado was searching for a chief financial officer.

After some research, I determined that the company was positioned to grow. So I decided to throw my hat in the ring.

While I had never been a CFO—I was only twenty-nine years old!—the title controller stood out prominently on my resume after working at the Rohling Inn. So, I sent my information to the president, Ken Schulz, and the owner, Gerry Reid, and began blowing the dust off my networks in my hometown.

I called Bob Tointon, the president of Hensel Phelps, a large construction company headquartered in Greeley. His son Bryan was a friend from high school and a groomsman in my wedding. Bob agreed to be a reference for me and actually called Ken on my behalf. Through Bob and some other connections, they offered me the position for a fairly modest wage. After discussing it with Trish, I accepted their offer and gave George Thompson my resignation letter, which was difficult because he had become a very good friend.

"What would it take to keep you here?" he asked.

"To be honest," I replied. "Nothing. This industry has worn me down. I'm ready for a change—and something away from the craziness here. It feels like the right thing."

We wished each other well, and off I went.

While I had earned an MBA with an emphasis in finance, the electronics manufacturing industry was completely new to me. No one at EFTC knew it (well, maybe a few), but I was in over my head. The first couple of years, I averaged about eighty hours a week. Most of my long days concluded in the bar mapping out business ideas and strategies on the back of cocktail napkins with my executive colleagues in the company. I was learning the ropes of the industry, how the books were being kept, getting to know our 160 employees, and nurturing relationships with people in the community.

Despite the stress of adjusting to my new job, I enjoyed reconnecting with the people I knew in high school and college. My position in a growing company also ushered me into the upper echelons of Greeley society (yes, it exists in Greeley!). I accepted a position on the board of directors of the University of Northern Colorado Foundation and rubbed shoulders with people like Dick and Charlie Monfort, owners of the Monfort Corporation and the Colorado Rockies baseball team; Dick Bond, president of the University of Northern Colorado; and

US senator Hank Brown. I also reconnected with my friend Tad Boyle, who worked as a stock broker for Dain Bosworth in Boulder. He eventually left the industry and became head basketball coach at the University of Colorado.

As my status in the community grew, so did my sense of pride and self-sufficiency. I was well on my way to becoming a self-made man.

My First IPO

Our company started doing very well with rapidly growing revenues and profits. The timing seemed right for taking the company public through an IPO (Initial Public Offering). It meant our company would be issuing publicly traded stock. This can be extremely lucrative if you offer a good product or service and your timing is right.

I was only thirty-one years old. Taking a company public was way beyond my capacity, but a couple of friends helped me navigate my way through it. Kevin Tice, my best friend and best man, worked at Salomon Brothers as an investment banker in New York and gave me very helpful advice. My friend Tad Boyle referred me to a lead investment banker from Dain Bosworth named Tom Heule. Upon my recommendation, our board of directors determined that Dain Bosworth was a good fit to take EFTC public.

Heading into early 1994, we positioned ourselves to take EFTC through an initial public offering. We were

going public! Needham & Co. out of New York and
J. C. Bradford out of Nashville co-managed the deal. We
hired a Denver law firm—Holme Roberts and Owen—
as our lead counsel. Together, we worked night and day
to prepare the documentation and the S-1 registration
statement, the initial registration form that is required by
the Securities Exchange Commission.

In early 1994, we began rehearsing our two-and-a-
half-week IPO road show presentation, where the team
travels to different destinations to sell stock to public
investors and mutual funds. As our rehearsals progressed,
though, tension began building between Ken Schulz and
Gerry Reid.

Gerry, the founder and owner, was a good man and a
country boy but was controlling, like many entrepreneurs.
Ken, the president, grew up in New Jersey, attended
Seton Hall, and was extremely bright and ambitious.
They complemented each other in business, but their
personalities were like oil and water at every level.

In late March 1994, we began our "dog and
pony show." The first week was certainly eventful as we
traveled from city to city, conducting anywhere from six
to ten meetings a day. Gerry gave an overview of how
the company was founded, Ken shared his vision where
the company was going, and I presented the financial
numbers and the analysis of future opportunities
that supported the valuation we were asking for the
stock.

After a week of traveling commercial, we all flew back home to Denver for the weekend. The tension between Ken and Gerry reached a breaking point, and to make matters worse, they lived across the road from each other. Late that Saturday evening, while we were back home in the middle of the roadshow, they reenacted a scene from *High Noon* on Reservoir Road, confronting each other in the middle of the road about the first week of the road show.

Their conflict seemed to clear the air. They avoided each other after that, which resulted in a much smoother week of presentations.

As we finished our trip, Dain Bosworth priced EFTC at eight dollars per share. Though it was a fairly small IPO compared to today's terms, $50 to $60 million of net worth was on the table, and the pressure of success or failure in light of a lifetime of work was at stake. We went to Rafferty's Bar and Grill in Greeley to celebrate. Drinking numerous Tanqueray Gin on the rocks and talking to our business leaders, I told everyone I was so excited I felt like a puppy dog that should be wearing a diaper.

Our stock started trading the next morning. Though not immensely wealthy, I suddenly had far more money than ever before. Instead of hunkering down and putting money in my kids' college fund or savings, I ordered a 1994 British racing-green Jaguar sedan with an XJ V-8 engine directly from London.

I wanted everyone to know that it was all about me.

After a month or two, the car showed up at the dealership in Denver. I couldn't get down there fast enough. "Finally," I thought. "The just reward for my talents and hard work." As I drove up to Stevenson Jaguar, I could see my dark green trophy sitting in the dealership parking lot.

After taking a quick look, I walked inside and found the salesperson, who escorted me back outside and opened the car door for me. As I sat down and inhaled, I was intoxicated by the heavenly aroma of the leather upholstery.

The sweet smell of success!

After signing the paperwork, I drove off the parking lot—and immediately the transmission went out. The dealership towed the car back for repairs. From that point forward, my green trophy was nothing but trouble.

Already, God was showing me the emptiness of the things of this world.

Trish and I used some of the money to buy a house on Boomerang Golf Course. I commissioned our contractor to build a full-service mahogany bar in the basement. This allowed me easy access to my alcohol reserves.

In our first year as a public company, we hit all the quarterly Wall Street analyst expectations, which pleased our investors. But by late 1995, growth began stagnating, and we needed a fresh vision.

Our board of directors was stacked with high-powered businesspeople like Bob McNamara, the managing director of Salomon Brothers in New York at the time, and Dick Monfort. While I wasn't a board member, I attended every meeting.

In late 1995, the board asked me to step out during one of our meetings. I walked across the hallway to my office and heard plenty of yelling and histrionics, but I couldn't tell what was going on. The conflict between Ken and Gerry had come to a head.

Change in Leadership

In a fairly dramatic move, the board fired Ken Schulz and placed Gerry Reid in the position of president. Then the board asked me, along with Gerry's wife, Lucille, to serve with Gerry in the newly created office of the president. So here I was, thirty-three years old, rising to the office of the president of EFTC. It was a big job and a lot of responsibility, given what was going on with the company.

I agreed to fill the position while the company searched for a full-time CEO. Although young and relatively inexperienced to be considered for that position, the board of directors felt I had enough leadership experience and acumen to step in and lead the company in the interim while EFTC looked for a president and CEO.

The board felt like we needed someone with a new vision and marketing background since we were pretty good at operations. After an extensive search, they offered the CEO position to Jack Calderon. Extremely bright, he had worked as Rosalynn Carter's press secretary when she was first lady. He also spent time as senior VP of marketing with Jabil, an electronic manufacturing company.

Because they bring wholesale change to the company (including the possibility of replacing the CFO), every new CEO presents inherent risk. However, Jack and I immediately hit it off personally and strategically, and we developed a long, deep friendship.

During my first meeting with Jack, I gave him a booklet I wrote with some ideas about moving the company forward. I assumed I was important enough that he should consider everything I said. He thanked me, put the book aside, and I knew at that point that he would never read it. He wanted to pursue his own plans.

In one of his first decisions, Jack named me to the EFTC board of directors. (This was before the Sarbanes-Oxley Act of 2002, which placed certain restrictions on naming CFOs to the board of a company.) So at a young age, I had already been given some prominent responsibilities and rubbing elbows with some titans of business.

While I was serving on the University of Northern Colorado Foundation Board, Trish and I were invited to a surprise party at the home of Dick Bond. When we walked in, we realized the surprise party was for Trish's and my ten-year wedding anniversary, which we were celebrating the next day. Senator Brown was present, along with some of the Monfort and Tointon families and others. It was quite a heady experience which only fed my pride and hunger for power.

At the end of 1997, the EFTC board decided to move our corporate headquarters from Greeley to Denver to be closer to Denver International Airport. Then we pursued an acquisition strategy to build the company. We purchased several manufacturing plants, or other electronic manufacturing companies, including OEM (original equipment manufacturing). Over the next two years, we conducted nine different mergers and acquisitions deals, and grew the company to nearly a quarter of a billion dollars of revenue, with about fourteen hundred employees.

My office in our new corporate headquarters sat next to Jack Calderon's on the top floor. In addition to being CFO, my responsibilities grew to include corporate strategic development and mergers and acquisitions. I spent a great deal of my time researching, buying, and selling companies and manufacturing assets. I flew an average of 250,000 miles a year during that time period.

We sold our house in Greeley and found a fifty-four-hundred-square-foot home for sale in Evergreen, just outside of Denver. The owner of the home was the president of the construction company that was building the Pepsi Center and Sports Authority Field (the new Mile High Stadium). The city of Denver demanded that he move within the city limits since the facilities were partially funded by Denver area taxpayers. His wife was not happy to have to sell their home.

I'll never forget the steely look on her face as she sat opposite us during our closing.

Another Season of My Discontent

By 1999, I was almost thirty-seven years old. Partly due to my efforts, EFTC boasted seven American factories, two international factories, fourteen hundred employees, and over $200 million in revenue.

Yet I felt a deep discontent.

Business was obviously going well. Like any company, we had encountered some ups and downs. Some of my acquisitions brought value to the company and some drained our resources. Our flawed acquisition of Allied Signal Manufacturing in Tucson, which I led, caused us to hemorrhage $5 million a quarter because we underpriced the deal. We ultimately sold the facility at a loss.

Nevertheless, I didn't feel Wall Street adequately valued our company. As the tech and communications bubble was starting to build, I felt that, given our revenue levels and earnings, our stock should be worth three or four times more than it was.

My record of success and burgeoning pride inflated my ego. I believed I could do anything, anywhere, with any company as a CFO, or if the opportunity was right, as CEO.

Bottom line: I wasn't getting rich as fast as I thought I deserved and could. I was chasing the gold.

Time for Another Change

By late 1999, while Trish and I were traveling in England on a business trip, playing golf in Scotland, and enjoying some of Great Britain's finest hotels, I decided to start looking for a CFO job in the tech industry that would reward me at a much faster pace. It may have been a short-term vision, but I felt the market was valuing communications and tech companies at a premium. Landing the right job could make me very rich. So, I put out feelers in the market that I was open to taking a new CFO or small company CEO job.

Howard Fisher Associates, a headhunter firm, called me about a small Seattle startup telecom company in the wireless industry. Metawave Corporation was looking for a CFO and wanted to take the company public. I agreed to a secret meeting with their CEO, Bob Hunsberger, at Denver International Airport.

Bob came to Metawave via Nortel, the multinational telecommunications company. He was very bright and in some ways a geek. Bob explained how Metawave's smart antenna technology would complement the growing cell phone industry (remember, this was still 1999). Despite his quirkiness, I immediately liked him—and he drove a Porsche.

"Stu," Bob explained to me. "We are on the verge of an explosion in wireless communication technology that is unlike anything the market has ever seen."

My eyes saw dollars.

"We are three months from filing our S-1 registration statement and taking Metawave Communications public. I'd like you to consider coming on board as our CFO. Your experience would lend great credibility to our executive team and convince investors that we have a solid public company leadership."

I couldn't have agreed with him more. Nothing could get in my way!

"Let me think about it, and I'll get back to you," I replied.

And *think* I certainly did. During that time, my disbelief in God began to grow. Authors like Bertrand Russell, Christopher Hitchens, and Sam Harris fed my growing atheism and watered the seeds of self-sufficiency which were planted in my life as a child. It was really all about me. In fact, in 1998, the *Denver Post* named EFTC the number-one public corporation in Colorado based on return on equity and stock performance. When the article came out, I read about our company and my success with a glass of Jack Daniels on the rocks in my hand, sitting in my mahogany walled office in Evergreen, Colorado. Needless to say, I was certainly proud!

Following my interview with Metawave's board of directors, in the presence of people like Bandel Carano, from Carano Capital, Bob Hunsberger, and founder Doug Reudink, I accepted their offer to become the Metawave's CFO and joined in early 2000.

After informing Jack Calderon of my resignation, EFTC board member Bob McNamara called me and said, "What can we do to keep you?"

"Nothing," I answered. "We've had a great run over the last eight years, but I want to move on from the electronics contract manufacturing world and try my hand at communications and technology products."

And with that, I said goodbye to some meaningful friendships and memorable experiences.

As we entered the new millennium, I set my sights on moving my family to Seattle and taking Metawave public in the dynamic telecommunications industry.

FOUR

CELL PHONES, TECH BUBBLES, AND TRANSITIONS

Just after the New Year I began learning everything I could about smart antenna technology and the wireless telecommunications industry. It was like drinking out of a firehose, but I knew they wanted to go public in the spring and I'd need to be ready to pitch investors by April. It wasn't until March that I first flew into Seattle and settled into a Residence Inn the morning before my first day of work. Trish would remain in Denver with the kids until summer break. Erich was ten and Hannah was eight. Sitting in my hotel room that evening I watched on television as demolition experts blew up the Kingdome, the Seattle sports stadium, to the ground.

"I hope the Kingdome blowing up is not a sign of how this new job in Seattle is going to go," I thought. "Metawave's public stock offering is only six weeks away."

Little did I know that my career would blow up like the Kingdome, but not with Metawave.

My first day on the job, I met with Bob Hunsberger and Doug Reudink. Everything felt so different from my experience at EFTC. Our corporate headquarters were located across the street from a golf course in Redmond, Washington, no more than a mile down the street from the Microsoft world headquarters.

I was the final piece of the executive team as we prepared to take the company through an IPO. They hired me because of my experience in successfully raising the money EFTC needed for their IPO. Our underwriters this time were Merrill Lynch, Solomon Smith Barney, and Piper Jaffrey, and we focused our sights on raising about $86 million.

Metawave had lost a cumulative total of over $100 million since their inception in 1997, and their revenue the previous year was only $22.6 million. But this was early 2000, as the tech bubble was reaching its height, when small companies barely generating revenues were finding investors willing to risk ridiculous amounts of capital.

My responsibilities at Metawave included overseeing the financials of the business as well as the operations (manufacturing and outsourcing the product). I made some wonderful friends at Metawave—Andy Merrill, our vice president of operations, Lowell Anderson, our head of engineering product management, and Kathy Surace-Smith our corporate counsel. Kathy's husband, Brad, was Microsoft's senior counsel and later became their president.

On the Road Again

It had been a grueling and intensive time to quickly learn more about the company, but I felt confident that I would be up to speed quickly in time for our road show in just a few more weeks, and that's exactly what happened.

My second road show looked much different than my first. This time, we traveled by private jet, both in the United States and in Europe, with limousines escorting us to our destinations. We conducted between six and ten meetings a day as we hawked shares of Metawave stock.

Halfway through the IPO road show the NASDAQ concluded its day with the biggest loss in its history. The NASDAQ was riding the wave of the tech and communications bubble reaching 5,133 points on March 10, 2000. By April 14, it dropped to 3,321 points, a loss of 35 percent from its all-time high a little more than a month earlier. It wouldn't surpass that number for another fifteen years.

Needless to say, our timing for the IPO road show was bad. But the show must go on, as they say, and it did. By the end of the two weeks, the underwriters had enough demand even in light of what was going on with the volatile market that the stock priced at nine dollars a share with a total corporate value of approximately $300 million.

I felt ebullient with the news, particularly given the difficult capital markets. Eight years earlier, in my executive capacity, I helped build EFTC. Then within months of arriving at Metawave, I helped take a company with only $22 million in revenue to a valuation more than EFTC had ever attained.

"Working for EFTC was the right decision," I thought, congratulating myself as I walked the trading floor of Merrill Lynch in Midtown Manhattan that day. "And moving to Seattle to work for Metawave was the right decision too." My company was going to be a big winner in the future because of the growth in wireless telecommunications—and I was going to enjoy riding that success as far as it would take me. The sky was the limit.

The next day, Doug, Bob, and I boarded the private airplane and flew back to Seattle and met some of our other executives, partners, and shareholders at Boeing Field to celebrate.

I felt strong and energetic. Only thirty-eight years old, and I had already taken two companies public. We had purchased a beautiful home in upscale Woodinville, Washington.

What could go wrong?

Then the Tech Bubble Burst

Over the next two years, we focused our resources on building our customer base with major carriers by selling them wireless network antennas and systems.

About a year after we took Metawave public, we were meeting shareholders in the Invesco Mutual Funds

office in Denver, when we learned a major earthquake hit
Seattle. Just before our meeting with the Invesco manager,
I snuck away to call Trish.

"Stu?"

"Trish, are you okay?"

"I'm fine. I was shopping at Costco when the
earthquake hit. The shelves were moving back and forth—
cans of food were raining down on us. It was terrifying."

"How are the kids?"

"They're fine. A little shaken up. The school followed
a drill, so they were prepared."

The earthquake was a precursor of things to come.
In 2002 a significant shift in the market caused the
telecommunications industry bubble to burst, particularly
in the area of new communications technology where
Metawave was positioned.

Many of the major cell carriers and their suppliers,
like Nortel and AT&T, were struggling to stay afloat
and avoid bankruptcy. During that time, Nortel's stock
dropped to sixty-seven cents per share, prompting many
of our customers to quit buying Metawave products
because we were a start-up company. Instead, they opted
to keep their major suppliers solvent by buying their
products.

Many long nights, I lay awake in bed asking myself,
"What should we be doing here? What are we doing
wrong? Why are we losing more and more money? How
many people should we be cutting? What direction should

we be taking the company? What should be our ongoing strategy?"

In light of all of the hardships in the telecommunications industry, I still felt confident we could solve the problems and make decisions in the best interests of the shareholders.

To medicate, I returned to my faithful companion—drinking. Every night when I walked through the front door at home, I poured myself a Tanqueray on the rocks and fretted over what was going on with the company. I was accustomed to being the wonder kid, the young prodigy who could solve any problem. But for the life of me, I couldn't outthink this one.

Because I worked sixty- to eighty-hour weeks, I had no friends and basically no support network. During that time I grew increasingly hostile to the Christian faith and the Christian worldview.

Trish, however, began walking a decidedly different path.

In 1998 while we were living in Evergreen, Trish met with Rev. Ken Williams, the senior pastor of Rockland Community Church in nearby Golden, Colorado. A friend of hers gave her the book *Left Behind* by Tim LaHaye and Jerry Jenkins, which tells the fictional story about Jesus returning to earth and taking his followers to heaven while leaving the rest of the world behind. As a nonpracticing Catholic, she didn't want to be left behind.

Trish presented a list of questions for Rev. Williams.

"If I become a Christian, can I still go to the Little Bear bar in Evergreen?"

"Of course you can still go to the Little Bear!" Pastor Ken answered.

"I'm not buying that God took out all the people on the earth during the flood, except for Noah and his family."

"Does the exact number of people who perished in the flood really matter compared to your eternal destiny?" Pastor Ken asked.

"How about this. I know that Jesus died on the cross for us, but why was that horrific death necessary? I didn't ask him to do that for me!"

"The Bible says the life is in the blood," he gently responded. "In the Old Testament, a sacrifice was always required for the forgiveness of sins. God gave Jesus, his one and only Son, as the ultimate sacrifice for your sins and to reconcile you with the Father.

"Trish, our women's retreat is this weekend. I encourage you to attend."

She left that meeting in tears and gave her life to Christ that weekend at the Rockland Community Church women's retreat.

Trish's Newfound Faith Actually Drove Us Apart

Rather than make our marriage better, Trish's conversion made our marriage worse because we were unequally yoked. In 2 Corinthians 6:14, the apostle Paul writes, "Do not be unequally yoked with unbelievers. For what partnership has righteousness with lawlessness? Or what fellowship has light with darkness?"

Trish began caring more and more about the things of God and loving others. I cared about worldly issues and my needs. Over time, we had little to nothing in common and argued about everything. Yelling and anger became the common currency in our home. Trish then decided to stay quiet whenever I was home, to keep me from getting angry and prevent arguments in front of the children.

During that time, significant issues surfaced between Trish and me. We were both fiscally conservative, but Trish was becoming more and more socially conservative, advocating for the unborn and people who were most vulnerable. I became more socially liberal and enthusiastically enlightened her about the errors in her thinking. Television programs containing violence and sex became abhorrent to her—I didn't care and controlled the remote. Trish wanted our children to know God, so she started sending them to vacation Bible school, Christian summer camps, and youth groups. I could not have cared less, so, if the kids balked about going, I gave her zero support.

After our move to Seattle in 2000, Trish began checking out some different churches, but didn't feel truly challenged until she found Mars Hill Church pastored by

Mark Driscoll. It changed her life and continued to move her down the path of a deeper faith.

Her spiritual awakening stirred my opposition to Christianity more and more. I demeaned her and her faith and tried to prevent her from going to worship or involving herself in the church community. I called her a Jesus Freak and Bible Thumper. I told her repeatedly that she had no balance in her life. At times, I even threatened her with divorce, but I couldn't follow through with it. Remembering the pain of my parents' divorce and my mother's subsequent relationships and multiple marriages prevented me from following in their footsteps. For the life of me, I couldn't understand why anyone would need God.

"Why don't you leave him?" Trish's friends asked her.

"I've scoured the Bible for any verse I can find that would give me permission to leave Stu," she responded. "But I can't find anything that applies to our situation." She felt God was telling her that he cared more about her holiness then her happiness. She stayed the course.

So, while my heart grew hard toward God, she continued to grow in her walk with Christ. I became more reliant on myself to rescue my family and keep Metawave afloat while Trish became more reliant upon God for hope and strength.

By late 2002, it was clear that Metawave was not going to make it. The tech industry had collapsed, at least in terms of raising capital. The telecommunications industry was focusing all of its purchasing power on keeping the larger manufacturers afloat, leaving tech start-ups like Metawave with few resources to survive.

I walked the company through their bankruptcy proceedings and resigned before the final filing. There was no need for me to stick around, as the company was saving money and preparing to unwind operations in a devastated telecommunications market. So by early 2003, I was unemployed and looking for my next role in the corporate world.

One Sunday during my job transition, Trish asked me once again to join her at Mars Hill Church. This time I said yes just to placate her. It was my first time listening to Mark Driscoll preach. I distinctly remember his sermon. He preached on predestination, the belief that God is sovereignly in control of every human decision and that He moves every event toward his ultimate purpose. I found the message extremely compelling—and infuriating. How dare he suggest that a deity exists with authority over my free will and personal sovereignty?

"Listen all you middle-aged men," Driscoll barked from the pulpit. "Are there things in the Bible that you don't agree with or understand? TOO BAD! You're not God!"

Sitting in the congregation, red-faced, it occurred to me that I couldn't wait to come back and hear him again. Something in his words struck me as true, though my truth did not line up with this fiery preacher's truth.

Working in Chicago, Living in Seattle

Landing my next position was a much higher priority for me then matters of faith. Soon after resigning from Metawave, I contacted Jack Calderon, the now ex-CEO of EFTC. He was working for a Chicago investment banking firm called Lincoln Partners, focusing on mergers and acquisition (M&A).

Jack concentrated his work in the electronic manufacturing and tech industry, both industries that I knew, so I asked if I could come out and see what he was doing and talk about the possibility of joining Lincoln Partners as an investment banker specializing in M&A deals. That meant our family would possibly move to Chicago.

Jack invited me to fly out to Chicago, so he could introduce me to the partners and other members of the team. The next day I caught a late-night Alaska Air flight.

During our meeting, Jack mentioned that he was looking for a vice president to do investment banking work in the electronics and technology industries. In my previous business dealings, I had already met the founders of Lincoln Partners, Rob Barr and Jim Lawson, who were still working there. The job seemed like an obvious fit.

Because the kids were in school, Trish and I agreed that I would commute from Seattle to Chicago. Every Sunday night, after a few cocktails to help me sleep, I boarded a red-eye to Chicago, (or other city to evaluate a company). I then rode the train (or a cab) straight to my apartment in the River North area of Chicago, showered, dressed, and went to work. Every week or two, I flew home on a late Thursday or Friday morning and spent two or three days with the family before repeating the routine.

When at home in Seattle, my life revolved around my kids' activities. Erich played basketball and Hannah was into dance and drama. I watched their games, recitals, and plays through Sunday night and then caught the red-eye to Chicago. Occasionally, Trish and the kids spent time with me in Chicago.

Needless to say, commuting to Chicago was hard on me and the family. Despite the commute, I was still putting in eighty to a hundred hours a week, building my client base in addition to the usual M&A work. Investment bankers are known for working long hours. At the end of the day, I often hung out at the bars on Rush Street if I was in Chicago and drank late into the evening. My unhealthy lifestyle resulted in significant weight gain. I reached 312 pounds at my heaviest.

The transition from being the decision-maker and an executive officer of a company to a consultant and advisor to companies didn't sit well with my ego. I wanted to be in charge and being a consultant, even with the title of investment banker, seemed below my experience and abilities. And when clients didn't take my advice, it frustrated me to no end.

On the home front, my marriage was a wreck and my kids seemed happier with me away from home. Living by myself more days than living with my family—paired with my heavy drinking—was a disaster. I was growing increasingly self-absorbed and moody while Trish was growing in her faith and relationship with Christ. It mystified me. In my prideful, self-sufficient mind, I couldn't understand why she chose a weak crutch like religion. Watching her read the Bible and other Christian books stoked the fire of my anger, and I grew verbally abusive. When she started attending a church small group, I came unglued.

On one of our anniversaries, I took Trish out to a very exclusive, high-end restaurant in Seattle called Canlis. Trish was prepared to make the best of the evening and at one point she took my hand, looked me in the eyes and said, "I love you."

"Seriously?!?" I responded. "I think you're a nutjob!"

Her countenance took a nosedive.

My drinking, anger, and long absences from home impacted my kids quite differently. Sometimes Erich would help lead me upstairs after I had passed out from too much drinking. On occasion, he undressed me, cleaned up my vomit, and put me to bed. One time Trish asked him how this was impacting him, and he said, "Everyone has too much to drink from time to time!"

Hannah, on the other hand, did not dismiss my behavior. She vacillated between fear and anger and lived in a perpetual storm of mental and emotional extremes. She sought acceptance and affirmation anywhere she could find it, becoming sexually active and using drugs at a very young age. Ultimately, she invested years in counseling trying to heal and forgive my sin. When I wasn't too busy with the kids' or just too exhausted, which was most of the time, I accompanied Trish to church on Sunday mornings. In late 2003, my heart started to soften. I decided it was time to meet Mark Driscoll. We met at his office, and after our greetings I jumped in right away.

"Mark, I've heard you preach. It's compelling." I said.

I then proceeded to tell him about me, my career, and my accomplishments. I didn't mention my family nor the fact that I wasn't a Christian.

Finally, at the end of our meeting he looked at me and said, "Stu I have something to say that might be troubling to you, but I suspect it may not bother you. "I think that you're one of the most narcissistic, self-centered, and selfish people that I have ever met."

Rather than be hurt by his comment, I thought to myself, "Yes! First again!" I was prideful about being prideful. "Well, if I'm going to be first, I might as well be first in those things as well."

I liked Mark. Still do. I liked his directness. And he said some difficult and hard things, but he didn't offend me at all. He made me think, and I enjoy people who tell it like it is. There was an air of truth and authority about him that I liked.

Moving on to Isilon

About that same time, I determined that I didn't want to spend the rest of my life in investment banking and M&A consulting work. I wanted to return to the corporate world, hopefully tech-related, where I could have more control and authority to make the decisions and build another business. Besides, it was time to work in Seattle. With the struggles in my marriage, I needed to direct my energies on our relationship and my family.

Providentially, while on an investment banking assignment in Seattle, I met Matt McIlwain, a venture capitalist whose company invested in another company that was on the cusp of dramatic growth. He offered to connect me with them.

In early 2004, demand for massive amounts of digital storage skyrocketed for rapidly growing companies like DirecTV, Comcast, and Kodak. Isilon Systems created software technology and system hardware that clustered low-cost, scalable, off-the-shelf disk storage. Through Matt, I met Isilon CEO, Steve Goldman. We hit it off immediately. I really liked his intellect and his vision for the company.

After a series of interviews with the venture capitalists at Isilon, including Atlas Venture, Sequoia Capital, and Madrona Venture Group, they offered me the CFO position and tasked me with helping create a business model around their technology, so we could turn Isilon Systems into a viable business.

I thanked Jack Calderon and Lincoln Partners for the opportunity to work with them. While I really enjoyed my colleagues, we all agreed that I was a fish out of water. I finished up a final M&A deal for them, and by March 2004 I was ready to join Isilon.

With my torrid travel schedule slowing down, I began attending Mars Hill with the family on a more regular basis. While still an adamant atheist, my heart was slowly softening, and Mark Driscoll's sermons were beginning to sink in. My heavy drinking continued, but I was gaining an appreciation for how this Christianity thing was affecting my wife.

In early 2004, I returned to the corporate world as the CFO of Isilon Systems, which took me in a direction I never expected.

FIVE

ISILON
AND THE "GREAT SIN"

Halfway through my forty-first year of life, I accepted my third and final CFO position. At the time, I didn't realize that my corporate career would soon take a dramatic turn. From my perspective, the sky was the limit.

I was entering my peak earning years with over a decade of experience in corporate leadership. The time was right to score big with a technology company. Without question, I *knew* (in my mind, at least) that Isilon Systems would be worth billions. Positioned on the frontier of digital data storage, my role in the company could produce wealth for my family that would last for generations. Additionally, I envisioned other opportunities for wealth creation in private equity and venture capitalism after hitting it big with this unique company. Financial independence, with the emphasis on *independence!*

Seattle, home of Boeing, Microsoft, and a struggling online bookstore called Amazon was enjoying its reputation as the hipster capital, and Isilon Systems, located in the trendy Queen Anne district, was primed to join their ranks. My job was to take an equally cool technology and figure out how to make a profitable business out of it.

Transitioning back into the corporate world felt very natural. The executive team, including CEO Steve Goldman and Isilon founder Sujal Patel, did their best to make me feel welcome and empowered. Through my previous business dealings, I already knew other employees. Unlike my first CFO job at EFTC, I was completely comfortable in the role this time and felt experienced and well equipped to take on the massive task of building Isilon Systems.

My first day on the job, in March 2004, I learned I was employee fifty-five. With the growing demand for cloud storage and digital content, the low number of employees wouldn't last long. Almost immediately, I began building a team to carry out the company's strategic plan.

Along with the role of financial oversight, my other responsibilities included product manufacturing and distribution, and hiring someone to lead it. My good friend John Briant, whom I knew at EFTC, seemed like the perfect fit. He interviewed for the job and accepted our offer for vice president of operations.

By late 2004, companies like Comcast and Ofoto (a Kodak photo storage company), began buying our products to test our clustered storage software and systems. With growth skyrocketing, our leadership team and board of directors began planning how to move forward. Our board already consisted of high-powered business executives like Greg McAdoo from Sequoia Capital, Barry Fidelman from Atlas Ventures and Matt McIlwain from Madrona Ventures. Steve Goldman then brought in some outside members, including Bill Ruckelshaus, the US deputy attorney general during the Nixon administration. If you're a history buff, you remember that Ruckelshaus was a casualty of the "Saturday Night Massacre" during the Watergate scandal. Bill lived in Seattle and was a highly regarded businessman who added credibility to the board.

Business Flourished while My Marriage Suffered

Nothing could be going better on the business front. On the home front, however, things were headed in the opposite direction. Trish continued to grow in her faith and I could do nothing to stop it. My constant criticism didn't prevent her from reading her Bible and involving herself in the Mars Hill Church community. She grew in her reliance on God, and I grew in self-sufficiency and pride. The widening schism forced us into living two separate lives.

But Trish continued to pray for me.

My heavy workload and drinking and growing hostility toward God concerned her. One shred of hope, though, kept her praying: I continued attending Mars Hill with her.

Now, Trish had an irritating—and endearing—habit. From time to time she left Christian books around the house that she wanted me to read. They usually involved theology or stories about men who found God. I rarely picked them up and read them. When I did, some of the books were downright funny to me. One book was about a man who moved away from his family to find himself, and he became a Christian while he was living in a cave. I laughed out loud and wondered, "Does she want me to find Jesus or go live in a cave?"

Despite—or maybe because of—my busy work schedule, my children flourished. Hannah embraced education; she absolutely loved to learn. To my regret, I spent virtually no time with her. When Erich was a freshman at King's High School, he earned good grades and started on the varsity basketball team. I *did* carve out enough time to watch Erich play basketball, but of course, I did so out of self-interest. I was living vicariously through him. Idolatry takes many forms, and the performance of a son or daughter is certainly one of them.

Both Erich and Hannah felt pressure from me to excel and make me proud. Erich knew that attending Stanford was on my mind—though not his. Hannah desperately wanted my approval, but more so, she wanted me. However, nothing stood in my way to succeed as a businessman. Success as a father and husband be damned.

In early 2005, Mars Hill Church opened up a video campus at King's High School, where my kids attended. It was closer to our house, which made it more convenient for me to join Trish at worship. I liked watching videos of Mark Driscoll preach because he didn't come across as churchy. I begrudgingly weathered the Christian music at the beginning of the service and left immediately following the sermon, before the service was finished. Trish was just happy that I joined her.

That year, we decided the kids would transfer back to public schools. Erich would transfer to Woodinville High School, a much bigger school, to play basketball and Hannah to Timbercrest Junior High. That same fall, a sophomore foreign exchange student from Syria moved in with us. Sami Alashi was a bright young man with a winsome character. We immediately hit it off.

Not coincidentally, Sami was also a Christian.

While I was intent on making as much money as possible as quickly as possible, Sami explained that his parents were both doctors—one an optometrist, the other a dermatologist —and that their combined income was twelve thousand dollars a year, a little more than a taxi driver earns in Damascus. He wanted to pursue his dream of becoming a doctor, but rather than creating wealth, serving others and glorifying God was Sami's goal. "What kind of warped perspective was that?" I thought.

During the year that he lived with us, he shared his faith with me openly and naturally. At Erich's basketball games, Sami would sit next to me and watch the game with great enjoyment. He would also watch amusingly at my histrionics and complaints about the coaching. "It's okay," he would say as he grabbed my arm. "Erich is playing great and God is in charge anyway."

"Yeah, yeah," I'd mumble and get back to watching the game.

Sami described to me the sacrifices Christians made while living in a Muslim-dominated country. Syria was 15 percent Christian, and generally, the Muslims tolerated the Christians. Remember, this was 2006, before the Syrian civil war devastated the peoples and lands of that great and ancient country. He explained to me that in Syrian schools they did not teach that Israel was a legitimate nation, and he had never heard of the Jewish Holocaust. He didn't believe it until I showed him some news articles on the Internet (which was blocked in Syria). That evening Sami and his parents had a long phone conversation, and in many ways I'm glad I was not able to understand the language.

Despite his young age, I found his authentic faith compelling and disarming. I also respected the sacrifices and commitment of having a relationship with Jesus Christ in a country where such faith could cost you your life.

After the school year, Sami returned to Syria, where he now works as a doctor. He remains one my favorite and most loved friends of all time. Looking back, I can see that even in that short time, he planted seeds of the gospel in my life.

IPO #3

By late 2005, Isilon began building momentum in the market. MySpace, Kodak, and Comcast were using our product as well as security companies and government agencies. Then NBC chose to use us for storage for the 2004 Summer Olympics. Obviously, the technology market and business community considered us viable and needed our innovative digital storage products, which accelerated our customer base.

We needed to raise more capital to continue the growth and our options were either another private capital raise or taking the company public. So I met with Steve Goldman and presented my idea.

"Steve, I've been thinking about the growth we're experiencing, and I don't need to tell you that we need an infusion of capital. In my opinion, raising private money is expensive and dilutive. I believe the best option for us is to consider a capital raise and liquidity event for our early shareholders by taking the company public."

"I completely agree with you," Steve replied. "What are you thinking?"

"Well, similar tech companies in the current market have been successful at raising the money they need through an IPO. Plus, the shareholders will be happy because it will increase the company's liquidity and bring a strong return on their investment. Additionally, I believe we'll be one of the hottest technology IPO's in years because of our unique market position and product offering.

"Isilon is ready to take the next step. We're growing. We're strong. And I've already done this before. Twice. Trust me on this, Steve. We can pull this off, and it's going to make for a great story on Wall Street!"

I could hardly contain myself. Back to being a puppy who needed a diaper. The board approved our proposal to go public, and I began working on my third IPO at the young age of forty-three.

In short order, I began assembling a team. Wall Street firms began advising us on which firms to include and which people could position us for success in the public market. I hired a new controller, Bill Richter, who brought vast experience in auditing. We also brought on a superb lawyer, Craig Sherman, and his firm, Wilson Sonsini, as our general outside counsel to help lead us toward the IPO. Doug Choi, whom I hired in the previous year, served as our internal general counsel. Then we enlisted high-powered Keenan Conder as our general counsel to build our investor relations management team. In the process, we realized that Isilon Systems stood a great chance of being one of the hot tech IPOs in recent history due to the growing need for massive amounts of digital storage.

I felt like a chess player moving my pieces in place to achieve a checkmate. My addiction to power and control invigorated me.

We outgrew our office space in Queen Anne, so we moved into a very hip, high-tech, almost spaceship-looking building in the Belltown area of Seattle. My corner office, situated on the top floor next to the CEO's, overlooked Puget Sound and West Seattle. When I wasn't hard at work, I could watch the whales swimming and snorting below.

Late spring 2006, we launched our dog-and-pony shows for Wall Street underwriting firms. Interested candidates in taking us public included Goldman Sachs, Morgan Stanley, Merrill Lynch, JP Morgan, Bear Stearns, and smaller tech firms like Needham & Co and Piper Jaffrey. We chose Morgan Stanley to be the lead manager with Merrill Lynch, RBC Capital, and Needham & Co. as co-managers. My close friend, Kevin Tice, who by this time headed Merrill Lynch's technology division, co-led on their behalf.

By the fall of 2006, we organized the company into numerous work group sessions. As CFO, I led the IPO process. The underwriters were going through a variety of drafting sessions with the management team. Price Waterhouse Coopers (PWC) conducted our internal audits.

Everything seemed to be on track and ready to go. Word on the street was that ours was going to be a very hot IPO. We registered about 8.3 million shares with an offering price of twelve to fourteen dollars a share and an additional 1.2 million shares of stock available in the case of an oversubscription—this is called the shoe in Wall Street parlance. All we needed to do was work through the SEC's comments, the final iteration of the S-1 registration statement for the prospectus and prepare for the road show.

The Morgan Stanley underwriters began setting up the mechanics of the domestic and international road show for a mid-November IPO kick-off. They decided we would travel by private G-10 jet, so we could fly to our destinations quickly. Limousines would then transport us to our meetings with the top institutional funds and investors in America and Europe.

A Heart of Flesh

In summer 2006, we decided to move the kids back to King's High School because of the Christian environment. Erich and Hannah loved the school, and though I wasn't sure exactly why, I felt it was the right place for our kids. This time, the move would be for good. And if we were going to do this, we would do it right. We sold our home in Woodinville and moved closer to the school, in Shoreline, to be part of the King's community. I didn't know it at the time but being surrounded by the Christian faculty and families most definitely impacted me.

Through my periodic attendance at Mars Hill Church, I met a man named Alan Artman. One Sunday morning at the Ballard Mars Hill campus Alan spoke about what God had done for him and what a growing relationship with Jesus looked like to him. The campus pastor who had referred me to Mark Driscoll in my first counseling session—Bill Clem—introduced Alan to the congregation by saying, "Alan is a CFO, which to a pastor means chicken fajita officer." I found the description hilarious. Then Bill interviewed Alan about his walk with Christ and some of his personal issues that he still struggled with—like drinking too much. I was shocked that Alan felt so comfortable talking about his life in such an open and authentic fashion. I liked Alan so much that I introduced myself to him that morning and asked to meet for coffee.

Later that week we met at Starbucks.

My initial questions were very tertiary.

"Hey Alan, can you tell me about your business? Tell me about your family. What accounting firm does your business use?"

Then I honed in on a few questions that prompted our meeting. "How did you get interested in Christianity and how do you feel so comfortable talking about Jesus in front of people? You mentioned your struggles with alcohol. Do you mind if I ask how you have overcome your drinking problem?"

He explained that he still struggled with drinking. I was struggling with that as well, and we hit it off.

"Stu, why don't you join me at our men's morning Bible study? We meet here every Monday morning at 6:30."

"Thanks for the invitation," I replied. "We're in the middle of an IPO, and I just don't have time."

While my lack of time was *a* reason for declining, my real reason was that I wasn't yet ready to take any additional steps into the Christian faith and community. Not coincidentally, Trish met Alan's wife, Pam, and started attending the same community group as the Artmans.

By the middle of 2006, I finally gave in to Trish's repeated quests to join her at her community group.

"Look," she pleaded. "I hate going by myself, and you already know people who go there. You told me you enjoyed getting to know Alan Artman."

"I'll go once," I told her. "But please don't make me sit through some kind of prayer session because I'll either fall asleep or get pissed if it goes too long."

People in the group ranged from college age to an eighty-year-old truck driver and his wife, and every background in between.

The community group met near the original Isilon corporate offices in the Queen Anne area, and though I felt uncomfortable at first, I really liked the people. They walked through life together, openly shared their lives with each other, studied the Bible together, and prayed for each other. I had never experienced anything like it, where men and women shared with such openness and honesty.

When they prayed, I refused to close my eyes and bow my head because I wasn't going to pray to a God that I didn't believe in. But I showed them respect and felt comfortable enough to enjoy the evening.

Subsequently, Trish asked me to go back numerous times, and I usually answered no. But I occasionally joined her and grew to like the people, particularly the old truck driver and his wife. I asked him questions about his life and his faith in God, and he always respectfully and gently answered them and engaged me in conversation. He was one of the wisest and smartest people I had ever encountered.

Alan Artman and I grew as friends as well. He was very transparent about his struggles, which unnerved me. It was the first time I'd been around a man who was so comfortable sharing about himself and his sins. Nevertheless, I wasn't ready to share about mine, which included my growing struggle with food and alcohol. At that point, I still weighed about three hundred pounds.

One morning while meeting for coffee, I took a significant step.

"Alan, I think I'd like try out your Bible study. Trust me, I'm not very religious, but I'd like to know more about what the Bible says."

"Trust me, I'm not religious either," Alan chuckled. "What!?" I thought to myself. "Didn't he get up in front of the congregation and talk about his Christian faith? That was very religious."

Though I didn't go every Monday, I wanted to see what transformed the lives of so many men who impressed me.

During that time, I started attending the community group with Trish on a more regular basis, which led to building relationships with people at Mars Hill. This made it easier for me to join her on Sunday mornings at the Mars Hill Shoreline campus. At times, I even stayed through the entire service.

One evening while Trish and I were driving somewhere, sitting at a stop light, I looked at her and said, "You know, I can actually feel my heart starting to soften." When Trish heard those words she leapt for joy internally but played it cool at the time. I hadn't accepted Jesus Christ into my life, but I could sense a growing comfort with her faith and the Christian faith.

I began spending time with men from the Bible study. And even though Mark Driscoll's sermons convicted me—and angered me at times—I wanted to hear more and more of what he had to say. I now look back and see that the Holy Spirit was wooing me into the arms of a real and loving God.

While my interest in the Christian faith continued to increase, so did my drinking. The stress of preparing to take Isilon public was overwhelming, so I increased my indulgence to "take the edge off." I realize now I was looking for any excuse I could find to crack open the bottle.

Just before leaving for the IPO road show in mid-November, I started reading the book *Born Again*, which Trish left on the table next to the bed. In it, Chuck Colson tells the story of his conversion after serving as the special counsel and hatchet man for Richard Nixon during Watergate.

Chapter 8—"An Unforgettable Night"—arrested me. I couldn't think of anything else. In it, Colson describes his conversion experience. As the government was applying pressure on him, he felt a growing sense of something lacking in his life. Tom Phillips, the CEO of Raytheon, gave Chuck a copy of C. S. Lewis's book *Mere Christianity*. The chapter "The Great Sin" dramatically impacted his life.

After finishing the chapter, I walked up to Hannah's bedroom and found a copy of *Mere Christianity* on her bookshelf. I found the chapter "The Great Sin" in section 2 of the book and was spellbound. The chapter, which addresses pride, described me! Four passages in various parts of the chapter particularly spoke to me:

> There is one vice of which no man in the world is free, which everyone in the world loathes when he sees it in someone else and of which hardly any people except Christians hardly imagine what they are guilty of themselves. . . . The essential vice, the utmost evil, is pride. Unchastity, anger, greed, drunkenness and all that are mere flea bites in comparison. It was through pride that the devil became the devil. Pride leads to every other vice. It is the complete anti-God state of mind. . . .

Pride is *essentially* competitive—is competitive by its very nature. . . . Pride gets no pleasure out of having something; only having more of it than the next man. We say that people are proud of being rich or clever or good-looking, but they are not. They are proud of being richer or cleverer or better-looking than others. If everyone else became equally rich or clever or good-looking, there would be nothing to be proud about. It is the comparison that makes you proud: the pleasure of being above the rest. Once the element of competition is gone, pride is gone. . . .

Pride always means enmity. It *is* enmity. And not only enmity between man and God, but enmity to God.

In God you come up against something which is in every respect immeasurably superior to yourself. Unless you know God as that— and, therefore, know yourself as nothing in comparison—you do not know God at all. As long as you are proud, you cannot know God. A proud man is always looking down on things and people: and, of course, as long as you're looking down, you cannot see something that is above you.

Lewis's words really shook me up, but I still wasn't ready to acknowledge the existence of a God or that I needed Jesus. After reading "the Great Sin" I reread portions of *Born Again* a day or two later and reflected on one particular passage. In it, Chuck Colson wrote that when he read the "The Great Sin" chapter in *Mere Christianity*, he wept in his car and felt the Holy Spirit speak to him:

> And then I prayed my first real prayer, "God, I don't know how to find you, but I'm going to try! I'm not much the way I am now, but somehow I want to give myself to you." I didn't know how to say more, so I repeated over and over the words: *Take me.*

> I had not "accepted" Christ—I still didn't know who He was. My mind told me it was important to find that out first, to be sure that I knew what I was doing, that I meant it, and would stay with it. Only that night something inside me was urging me to surrender—to what or to whom I did not know.

> I stayed there in the car, wet-eyed, praying, thinking, for perhaps a half an hour, perhaps longer, alone in the car in the quiet of the night. Yet for the first time in my life I was not alone at all.

After reading Colson's words, I did not pray, but it became clear to me that for the first time in my life that, like Chuck Colson, I was not alone.

Preparing to leave for the IPO road show, the words of C. S. Lewis and Chuck Colson haunted me. Like a song that gets stuck in your head, I couldn't escape their words which both disturbed and comforted me. I was gaining a growing understanding of the potential of a living and loving God in the world and my life, but I continued to fight that idea because it wasn't consistent with the worldview I lived with for the first forty-three years of my existence.

I hoped the road show would distract me from my inner turmoil, but it didn't.

SIX

PUBLIC AND PRIVATE OFFERINGS

The morning of November 27, 2006, a luxury G-10 twin jet engine plane greeted Isilon CEO Steve Goldman, our VP of marketing Brett Goodwin, and me at Boeing Field as we launched our two-and-a-half-week road show. Welcoming us aboard were two pilots, a personal flight attendant, a plane full of food, and all the liquor we could drink.

I didn't pack heavy, just a suit, some shirts, and the essentials. If I needed some laundry done, the hotel would do it. We agreed to return to Seattle every weekend before our December fourteen public offering.

Most road shows begin with the smaller fund companies in the Midwest in order to work out the bugs before meeting with the biggest financial managers in the country in Boston, New York, and Los Angeles. We started in Kansas City by meeting with the investment bankers from Morgan Stanley.

Steve Goldman kicked off each session by introducing Isilon and painting a vision for the dreams and direction of the company. Brett followed Steve by briefly explaining our technology. Then I presented the financials—income statement, balance sheet, cash flow—and offered some basic revenue forecasts. Finally, the portfolio manager (PM) and their analysts would ask a variety of questions and the session would conclude with the three of us attempting to answer their questions. This often involved some lively and sometimes intense dialogue and insights that could become competitive and certainly intellectually challenging.

Participating in a road show isn't a walk in the park. Our days were long and intense, starting early in the morning with a quick workout, if there was time, and then on to a breakfast meeting with groups of investors in a hotel conference room or at their corporate offices. After breakfast, our stretch limousine whisked us off to the next series of meetings. The number of meetings we held depended on the number of quality money managers in that city. When those meetings were done, we headed to the airport and jetted off to the next big city. We averaged eight to ten meetings a day.

Portfolio managers are some of the smartest people in the world. Many have earned their PhDs from institutions like Oxford and MBAs from Harvard and Stanford. They can also be some of the most difficult and demanding personalities as well, so we knew what to expect when meeting with the PMs from bigger money management companies like Fidelity, Invesco, or large pension funds.

Nevertheless, entering my third IPO, I was undeterred. Going mano a mano with the best and brightest, interacting with their challenging personalities and taking on their most difficult questions energized me.

Assessing a road show midstream can be difficult. A portfolio manager may seem enthusiastic about our stock and then never place an order. On the other hand, some of our seemingly worst and most difficult meetings resulted in a ten percent order of the entire offering. This time around, our meetings with investors seemed very positive, and our investment bankers confirmed this.

Following our last set of meetings in Los Angeles on the evening of Wednesday, November 29, we flew back to Boston. After three full days of meetings under our belts and with another two long days ahead in the Northeast before going home, everybody was tired. That night, I looked out the window of our G-10 as we flew across the country and watched the half-moon cast light on the clouds below. After a few Tanqueray's, I reflected on all the road shows I had done. Despite the excitement that our presentations were generating, I felt melancholy, bored and unfulfilled. Considering my success having done this IPO thing a few times, I should have been excited and content, but I wasn't.

Something was amiss emotionally and spiritually as I considered my lot in life.

On the Verge of Something Big

The next day in Boston we held ten meetings with some of the biggest investors in America. By the end of the intense day on Thursday, we realized this could be a very hot technology IPO. Four years after the telecommunications and technology bubble burst, we felt our company might be *the* company to break through the barriers and bring the industry back to the good old days of the late 1990s. That evening, we flew to New York and spent the night at the Plaza Hotel.

Friday morning, while walking the Manhattan streets to our next meeting, I noticed Steve Goldman talking on the phone. He glanced at me like they were talking about me. He attempted to give me a comforting nod and then he looked away. The concern on his face told me something was amiss. After he hung up the phone, I was curious about the conversation. As we strolled down Park Avenue in Midtown Manhattan the awkward silence told me something was on Steve's mind. Finally, after a few minutes I mustered the courage to find out what was on his mind.

"What's up?" I asked Steve.

"Oh, I don't know," he said. "That was Bill Ruckelshaus." He was a member of our board of directors. "He told me the board received a letter from a member of our in-house legal team about your blow-up over the S-1 registration statement the other day. Apparently, he told them you yelled at him because he couldn't find a way of listing you as one of the company's five highest-paid employees.

"He's concerned because your anger hurt his feelings, and he felt that you were running hot about not being listed. He feels you're emotionally on edge and, frankly, abusive to him.

"Stu, to be honest with you, if I had my choice, I'd prefer not to have my compensation listed publicly because I don't want everyone knowing what I get paid, or anything else private for that matter."

"Look," I blurted out to him. "First of all, that guy is a momma's boy, and he's out of his league given where our company is going. That conversation was supposed to be just between him and me. But I still stand by what I said. Most people couldn't do what we're pulling off, and the idea that the CFO of Isilon is not one of the five highest paid people in the company pisses me off. I want everybody to know what I'm making because I work hard for it.

"Look Steve, you can be guarded about what you make, but g****** it, I deserve every penny I've earned. What we're doing on this road show and the value we've built with this company is making all our employees and shareholders rich!"

"Granted," Steve answered. "Stu, your opinion, though overblown and frankly offensive to most people, may have a ring of truth, and I respect you. Nevertheless, the man complained that he felt intimidated by you. You need to keep your emotions and your opinions about him and your compensation to yourself. Do you hear me?"

"Yep." A long silence followed us as we walked down the thriving street.

"Hey, Steve," I said.

"Yeah." He looked at me.

"The guy is a p****." I blurted out. We both laughed so hard tears ran down our faces.

As the laughter died down, we walked down the road to the next meeting in Manhattan, and I felt a sense of irony and discomfort about the conversation. I remembered Chuck Colson's and C. S. Lewis's words from the previous week about pride being the great sin. While I didn't feel overwhelmed with conviction or even regretful about what happened, I *could* admit that my pride caused the confrontation with the in-house lawyer and the subsequent call from the board members.

After concluding our meetings that week, we debriefed in the mahogany offices of Morgan Stanley in Midtown Manhattan. Paul Kwan, the lead Morgan Stanley investment banker on the Isilon System IPO, and Rob Kindler, the Morgan Stanley vice chairman of investment banking sat in the meeting and seemed exuberant.

"Gentlemen," Paul started out with a hint of formality yet a satisfied tone of familiarity with his Isilon executive team in his voice. "You are knocking the cover off the ball in these meetings. Numerous people in the field are interacting with the PMs of the various money management firms you've met with. We are getting a sense that the book of orders is going to build nicely. Not to get your hopes up, but I think this offering could be fifteen to twenty times oversubscribed."

"All we need you guys to do is the same thing you're already doing," Rob Kindler chimed in. "Our job is to get you to the meetings on time, and not lose the management team while we're on the road."

After about forty-five meetings our first week, we were off to a great start. The underwriters Morgan Stanley, Merrill Lynch, RBC Capital, and Needham were hearing very positive feedback from the portfolio managers, analysts, and fund investors.

That evening, we flew back to Seattle and arrived late. Trish picked me up from the airport—which was a good thing since I had already downed five or six drinks on the airplane and was in no condition to drive. I looked forward to spending the weekend at home with my kids and watching Erich play one of his first basketball games of the season. I spent the rest of the weekend resting and rejuvenating for the upcoming couple of weeks leading to the conclusion and pricing of the Isilon Systems IPO.

Early Monday morning, we boarded a plane, flew over the North Pole, and landed in Amsterdam that night. The next two days, we met with money managers in Amsterdam, Munich, Berlin, and Frankfurt. Then we flew to London that evening. Like my night flight the previous week, the down time on our luxurious G-10 jet made room for that gnawing sense of melancholy to fester.

As the full moon shined in all its glory over the English Channel, I sipped on my Tanqueray on the rocks with an onion and reflected on my life. "Was this all there is to finally make it big in the corporate world?" I thought. "I own 450,000 shares of Isilon Stock options. If the stock grows to twenty dollars a share, like many think it will on the first day of trading, will an additional $9 million dollars really add meaning to my life? What if the price rises to a hundred dollars a share? Will having $45 million make me a complete person? Maybe $450 million will make me something that I haven't even realized? Has all the work leading up to this point in life given me a purpose that is meaningful?"

I remembered hearing a verse at the men's Bible study back in Seattle: "For what will it profit a man if he gains the whole world and forfeits his soul?" (Matthew 16:26).

Emptiness over the English Channel. Mahogany paneling, leather seats, and a private flight attendant be damned. It meant nothing to me. At least I had my gin. If my third IPO made me feel worse, not better than my first two, what could I look forward to in the future that would add real meaning? Something needed to change.

And the next day it would.

After landing at Heathrow Airport, a limousine whisked us away to downtown London, where we stayed at the luxurious Savoy Hotel. I went directly to bed, exhausted because I was unable to sleep on the flight to London.

The next morning, after a light breakfast, we began a series of nine meetings for the day. Afterward, all of us enjoyed a long dinner replete with an endless supply of cocktails and wine at an Indian restaurant in the trendy Soho area of London. Around 9:00 p.m., we left the restaurant to return to our hotel.

Walking the streets of Soho, we passed an older-looking office building that could have served as an apartment house. An investment banker with Morgan Stanley stopped us and pointed to a yellow star in the office window.

"See that?" he said, pointing to the star. "In that office, Karl Marx wrote his *Communist Manifesto* to the German Workers Educational Society that was used as a rallying document for an uprising of workers. That window and room, right there, is part of the birthplace of Communism."

"Lucky for us, Karl Marx didn't get it right, or we wouldn't be here," a voice piped in from our group. Everyone laughed. The irony of walking by the edifice in the midst of our road show didn't escape us.

"True," a member of our party chimed in. "But he did get one thing right. Religion *is* an opiate for the masses. It's nothing but a support for people's insecurities. A crutch."

"That's right," one of the members of our party echoed. "If it wasn't for religion, most of the wars in this world would have never taken place. Think of all the lives that would have been saved. If it wasn't for religion this world would be a much better place."

"Makes sense," I mumbled as I nodded my head. They continued their conversation as I listened. Then we headed back to the Savoy in our limousine.

During our ride, I thought about the many sermons I'd heard at Mars Hill Church. I reflected on Charles Colson's book *Born Again* and C. S. Lewis's comments about the great sin in *Mere Christianity*. I even thought about some of the things I had read and heard in the men's Bible study and Trish's community group back in Seattle.

"You all right, Stu?" Brett asked, disrupting my train of thought.

"I'm fine," I reassured him. "Just a little tired."

When we arrived at the hotel, Steve announced he was going straight to his room. Brett and Paul were heading to the lounge.

"Want a nightcap?" Brett asked.

"No thanks," I replied. My refusal was wholly unfamiliar to them given my penchant for nightcaps up to this point on the roadshow. "I'm going straight to bed. Still trying to shake the jet lag and the busy day."

A World Without Christ?

Entering my hotel room, I felt clearheaded—more clearheaded than normal—and I looked down at the wet bar. I had fully intended on having another drink or two before heading to bed, but instead I shook my head and sat down in a large oak chair with lambskin upholstery. Something was stirring in my gut, and more important, in my heart. I couldn't get the conversation about religion being the opiate of the masses out of my mind. It amused me because of how shallow and sophomoric the comment seemed, and yet it bothered me too. My mind in some ways wanted to say yes, but my heart said no.

Then a question reverberated deep inside. "What would the world be like without Jesus Christ?" I wrestled with the question and couldn't shake it. "Sure, the world is a broken and depraved place where wars and violence are commonplace," I thought. "Sure, there is suffering and endless heartache apparent everyday almost everywhere. But, what would the world be like without Jesus Christ?"

Sitting in that luxurious chair in that dimly lit hotel room, I reflected on the high points and the low points of my life. My quest for autonomy and self-sufficiency. My quest for freedom even as I was becoming more enslaved to the things of this world. My success and pride as a basketball player. The pain of my parents' divorce, and the way people who called themselves religious turned their back on my mom. Quitting the basketball team as a freshman in college because I wasn't getting enough playing time. Oh yes, the great sin of pride I'd read about in Colson's and Lewis's books. A predominant theme of my life. Waves of memories and pain washed over me.

I thought about my claim of being an atheist. My growing ability to argue a position of atheism. That worldview seemed to require more and more blind faith every day as I read the Bible and spent time with those who had a relationship with Jesus Christ. Did my views concur with Marx?

Then Trish came to mind. What would her life be like without Jesus? She was a much better person than me but being better wasn't her concern. Her joy seemed to come from something that she realized she didn't earn. Being better wasn't her goal; having a relationship with Jesus was her focus. How could she be joyful in anything if she didn't earn it? That's not how I saw life. Good things must be earned or they're not good. Where did that point of view arise in my life? Trish's belief in Jesus transformed her life for the better. Was religion an opiate to her? Trish was less interested in making war in our house and only in conveying the peace that seemed to come without any understanding. It didn't make sense.

Then, as I was prone to do, I thought about me. In the midst of our road show, I realized up to this point in my life that in any spiritual matter I had invested all my intellectual wares into the idea that God didn't exist. Because if he did, where did that leave me? I put all my stock in my*self*—my self-sufficiency, pride, abilities. There it was again—the great sin that propelled me throughout my life.

What *would* the world be like without Jesus Christ?

I looked at the clock and realized I had been lost in thought for two hours. Glancing at the wet bar fridge, I thought, "Maybe I should have a drink or two. No, not tonight." I didn't want anything to cloud my thinking. Plus, at least for that moment, the desire wasn't there.

Continuing my musing, I wondered about the many Christian people I had met at King's High School, our community group, and the men's Bible study. Was religion an opiate for them? They were far happier and experienced far more peace and joy in their life than me.

Mark Driscoll's sermons came to mind. His fiery persona was attractive, but what was more attractive was the truth that seemed to pour from his mouth in the pulpit. "You're not God!" "It's not about religion, it's about relationship—with Jesus!" "Good things that become God things become bad things." "The Bible is not about you, it's about him—a compassionate God who loves you deeply." "If you are not a Christian, you are headed into the path of God's wrath!"

Was entering into a relationship with Jesus Christ an opioid? Yeah, the world's broken; yeah, the world's depraved, but what would the world be like without Jesus Christ?

My Life *with* Jesus Christ?

Suddenly, I felt a warm wave of energy surge through me, and my eyes welled up with tears. I couldn't stop it. The tears rolled down my face. A feeling of joy but also a feeling of regret. A feeling of deep and unending love but a deep sense of the need to repent. What had I been thinking about? It seemed like a light came on, but the room was still dark.

"I've had this all wrong," I thought. "Yes, the world is a broken, depraved place. Yes, the world is violent and full of people who will pridefully fight for their own darkened opinions. What was happening here? It's like a light has been turned on. Wait a minute, the Bible says that Jesus healed people. He transformed people. He forgave people. He hung out with the worst of all people. He fought against those who are religious to have relationship with them. He was the only means to connect people to Father God."

Then I felt a divine presence in the room. Shivers ran up and down my spine. The Holy Spirit was there.

"Jesus," I cried out. "I have been so wrong! Religion may be an opiate for the masses, but a personal relationship with you is what I desire. I've worshipped myself, but it's empty. I don't want to live another moment apart from you. I give my life to you. Please forgive me of my pride, the great sin. Change me. Make me a better husband, a better father, a better man. Lord, make me one of yours and adopt me into your family."

I laid down on the floor on my face before God and sobbed all night. Every tear washed away a memory of rebellion, a harsh word, an indiscretion. I needed to be clean, so I let it all go. It didn't matter if people in the hallway or next door could hear me. I wanted to be cleansed of my self-sufficiency, machismo, pride, and career aspirations that were rooted in destructive self-focus. I wanted a relationship with Jesus Christ.

Much of what I thought about was how wrong I had been about Jesus. I felt remorse that I had spoken against him and persecuted my wife for having a relationship with him. I repented of those things and many more things. I wanted *him* to be in control. My tears of remorse then became tears of relief. The longer I prayed, the more empowered I became by a new sense of freedom, liberation, and forgiveness of my many sins.

From Wall Street to the Well

At that moment I felt like the Samaritan woman at the well in John chapter 4.

For centuries, Jews and Samaritans were at odds with each other. The product of intermarriages of the Assyrians and Israelites, Samaritans were considered heretical half-breeds by their Jewish cousins. The Jews worshipped *Yahweh* (God) in Jerusalem. Samaritans worshipped *Yahweh* (God) in the capital city of Samaria. Jews upheld their faith's strict dietary laws, Samaritans ate pork.

The two groups avoided all social contact. They didn't intermarry. They didn't trade with each other. They didn't even step foot on the soil of the other country. If their paths crossed it would not be unusual for hostility to break out.

In a very patriarchal time, Jewish men were known to say, "I would rather be a woman than a Samaritan." For good reason, the Samaritans hated the Jews in return.

One day Jesus decided to pass through the country of Samaria on his way home to Galilee. He stopped in a town called Sychar and encountered a Samaritan woman at the village well. Without hesitating, he asked her to give him a drink. Samaritan women at that time drew water from a well at the beginning and end of the day. Because the woman was alone at the well in the middle of the day means she was probably an outcast among the other Samaritan women. We learn that she had been married five times and was now living with a man who wasn't her husband. You can't get much lower than that.

Nevertheless, Jesus treated her no differently than he would a fellow Jew. *He asked her to give him a drink from the same bucket that she drank from.*

As her eyes meet the Lord Jesus, he sees within her a cavernous aching, a cistern in her soul that will forever remain empty unless he fills it. The woman didn't seek Jesus out in search of forgiveness. She came to the well for water, and Jesus pursued her! Not only that, but he also divulged to her that he was the Messiah, the first time he admits this to anybody.

Jesus' encounter with the woman tells us that regardless of past mistakes, hurts, pain, and failures—Jesus wants to fill us with his love because he sees intrinsic value in every person. Even the Samaritan woman at the well.

Even me.

That night in London, I knew I was no better than that woman. An impatient, arrogant, self-sufficient, greedy man with a penchant for booze. Nevertheless, I knew that Jesus loved *me*. Jesus died for *my* sins.

Into the early morning, I laid on the carpet while God washed me clean. Filthy rags made clean by the blood of the Lamb. Over and over, I prayed, "Lord, I'm yours. I'm yours. Just make me yours."

I had no idea where my life would go from there, but I was halfway through the road show for one of the hottest technology IPOs in four or five years in America. But instead of feeling prideful, for the first time in my life, I felt like I wasn't in this by myself or for myself.

It was a joyous and indescribable feeling, and it was a night that changed my life forever. A night that was etched in the Book of Life from the foundation of the world.

Little did I know that this change would affect my life in such a dramatic way.

SEVEN

FROM ARROGANCE
TO HUMILITY

Early the next morning, I got up off the floor of the Savoy Hotel, showered, put on a clean shirt and suit, and met our Isilon team in the lobby to catch a limo to our first breakfast meeting of the day. For going without sleep the night before, I felt surprisingly refreshed and energized.

No one mentioned our conversation the previous night in front of the Karl Marx building, and I said nothing about my encounter with Jesus Christ in my hotel room. We set off for London to meet with prospective institutional investors in a series of packed morning meetings. After our breakfast meetings, we hosted a lunch group presentation at a local hotel. While the investors consumed rubbery chicken and overcooked vegetables, we presented the Isilon story. Following that presentation, Barry Fidelman from Atlas Ventures, one of Isilon's earliest investors and a member of Isilon's board approached me. (He happened to be in London on business.)

"Are you okay? You seemed different in your presentation."

"I feel fine, just a little worn out from the road show." I did feel fine, but I was already sensing a shift in priorities, from my responsibilities on the road show to my prior evening experience.

After enjoying the weekend back in Seattle with our families, only three more days stood between us and the initial Isilon stock pricing on December 13 when the syndication manager would determine our opening stock price. But those final three days were going to be intense. We were flying to Boston and then New York City to meet with some of the biggest institutional investment firms in the world. Then the underwriting team would work hard with the Morgan Stanley syndication manager to allocate shares to institutional investors interested in being Isilon shareholders.

When I was home over the weekend, I found myself praying in secret. I wasn't ready to tell Trish about my experience in London because I was concerned about how it would impact my career. I also found myself asking God to keep the market stable and prevent any last-second events from occurring in the capital markets. Often, at the last second, something will happen in the broader market, causing it to drop that preempts companies in the middle of IPOs from going public.

That Sunday I attended worship with the family, and Pastor Mark's sermon took on new meaning. His fiery expository presentation of Scripture created a sense of joy and meaning, different than any time in the past. Instead of departing in anger and filled with questions, I left the sanctuary with a sense of peace and understanding.

Early on Monday, December 11, the Isilon team met at Boeing Field and boarded our jet for Boston for a day of meetings, landing around midday. A limo then escorted us to a series of afternoon meetings. That evening we flew to New York city to prepare for a final series of meetings before the pricing meeting with Morgan Stanley, Merrill Lynch, and the other co-managers of the offering. On Wednesday night, we met for dinner at Aureole Restaurant in midtown Manhattan with leaders of our investment banking team to discuss how the book of investors was coming together, how the pricing discussions may go, and the conclusion of the IPO road show and initial day of Isilon stock trading on the NASDAQ.

It Was Going to Be *Really* Big

We were getting a sense that the book—the shareholders who wanted to buy stock—was coming together, and it was going to be significantly oversubscribed. Some of the hottest IPOs in America will be as much as ten to twenty times oversubscribed, meaning that the demand for stock is much greater than the number of shares offered. That, of course, drives up the price of the shares, both in the initial offering price and the price in open market trading. The syndication team, led by

Morgan Stanley, told us this was going to be significantly oversubscribed, but we didn't know by how much.

In the late afternoon of Thursday, December 14, after some morning meetings, we met in the Morgan Stanley mahogany-laden conference room with the director of syndication, the director of investment banking, and the lead investment banker to discuss the opening price of Isilon's stock and to determine how much capital the company would receive in our bank account from the stock sale. While everyone else felt excited, tense, and a little anxious, I felt calm because I had been there before. Additionally, so much had changed in my heart that this pricing meeting felt less important and stressful than other meetings in which I had participated.

Pricing meetings are always tense because during that time, the syndication director for the lead bank recommends the stock price for all the underlying investment firms committed to an initial investment of the IPO shares. Corporate board of director members may argue for a higher price because it can generate greater amounts of money from the stock sale. Emotions are high because money is at stake. Pricing the stock too high may result in fewer takers and less momentum in the after-market for stock appreciation for new investors. But if you price it too low, the company leaves money on the table.

The syndication manager told us that the IPO was significantly oversubscribed. They wouldn't tell us exactly how much, but we knew it was somewhere in the neighborhood of fifteen to twenty times oversubscribed. That meant we would price at the upper end of the S-1 registration stock price filing range, or even above that. He recommended we set the opening price at thirteen dollars per share, with an expectation that there would be some upside on the first day of trading.

We gathered our underwriting pricing committee together with our board of directors pricing committee via telephone conference call. The Morgan Stanley syndication director explained the justification for the stock price, and Steve Goldman and I led the discussion with the board of directors, rationalizing why we should set the price at thirteen dollars per share. Extra shares called an over-allotment or greenshoe were available for sale if the demand at $13 per share was high. The syndication director told us they expected that at thirteen dollars per share, the over-allotment would sell out. So while we initially expected to raise somewhere in the $80 to $85 million range, with the sale of the over-allotment we would raise over $100 million in IPO proceeds that could be used to grow the company.

Everyone agreed that the stock price would be set at thirteen dollars per share. The stock would start trading on the NASDAQ the next morning, Friday, December 15, and after standing on the trading floor on Friday morning, our Isilon team would hop on the G-10 jet and get back to Seattle for our employee IPO party on Friday evening.

Thursday night we held our closing party—a huge celebration with a fancy dinner. Then afterward, a group of the investment bankers and I went out for a good time. We indulged in some debauchery, which included a visit to a Westside Manhattan strip club where we spent a bunch of money and drank high-end booze, which was not uncommon for a closing party for Wall Street men with growing wealth.

This time, however, my heart just wasn't into celebrating as heartily; my spiritual encounter and salvation in London changed my perspective and softened my heart. After realizing my ambition of taking companies public— and this one was a really big IPO—I knew something bigger and far better awaited me, though I didn't know what and felt some fear and reservation about what that might be.

The limousine dropped me off at my midtown hotel that night. I expected to see a strong opening day of trading the next day. I went to bed ready for the initial day of trading starting at 9:30 a.m. on Friday, December 15.

Vanity of Vanities

The next morning, the limo picked up the Isilon team from our hotel and drove us to the midtown Manhattan trading floor of Morgan Stanley. I was still a little hungover. We were going to stand on the trading floor as the momentous day began. In a few moments, Isilon's stock was going to open at thirteen dollars per share, and we would watch the stock price fluctuate in value on its first day of public trading until it made us wealthy.

With over 400,000 shares of stock options, many of them already vested, I was about to become a wealthy man in the world's eyes. After taking a tour of the Morgan Stanley trading floor, the opening bell rang at 9:30 a.m. Eastern time. Isilon's stock opened at $13 per share and immediately began a steady climb, peaking at almost $27.50 per share, more than double its offering price. Isilon team members spent the rest of the day hugging and congratulating each other. By the end of the day, the stock closed at $23.10, giving Isilon Systems a market value of $1.4 billion. My net worth was now around $10 million on paper. But something just didn't feel right, and I recognized that it had to do with my changing priorities. As I stood on the trading floor, I reflected on the fact that this was the third company I'd taken public as a CFO. I felt some satisfaction, but I didn't feel exuberant. First, I had been there before—although not at that level of wealth or importance. While my Isilon colleagues felt ebullient and optimistic, the sense of satisfaction, pride, and triumph all around didn't ring true with me. While many CFOs would feel elated, I felt an overwhelming sense of melancholy and dissatisfaction with what was happening—something that nagged me during each IPO, but this time the feeling was more intense. After coming to faith in London, I realized there was something bigger and more important to me than the Isilon IPO. My heart had changed, and I hungered for a relationship with God and his Word. I questioned my purpose and where God was going to take me for the rest of my life.

Some of the Morgan Stanley guys came up to me and gave me a hug.

"You okay?" one of them asked.

"I'm fine. Just worn out." Truth be told, I was already thinking about the long grind of building a public company. Our work was just beginning.

We left before the end of the trading day and flew back to Seattle. Later that evening we would join our employees for a joint IPO and holiday party in Belltown. Isilon had good reason to celebrate.

The flight from New York to Seattle dragged on and on, so to pass the time, I guzzled numerous Tanqueray martinis and looked out the window thinking, "Is this really what life is about? What am I going to do now?" After accomplishing my life's ambitions of taking companies public and becoming a multi-millionaire (on paper), I didn't know where to go from there in light of my internal conversion.

Trish picked me up from the airport and we headed straight to the restaurant. She congratulated me for the success of the IPO, but she, too, had been through this before. Trish could tell that something was on my mind as we rode together to the restaurant, but she let me look out the window in peace—plus, she could smell the gin on my breath.

When we arrived, the place was jovial. People congratulated me when I entered the restaurant, patting me on the back and thanking me for helping make them wealthy. I muscled up a smile and tried my best not to act as drunk or as melancholy as I felt. Our road show team addressed the employees, congratulated each other, and told some stories from our travels. I spoke from the balcony above the employees in the restaurant as everyone laughed and cheered. The evening was a huge success. I continued to drink more than necessary, and Trish drove us home, again mostly in silence as she sensed that something was on my mind.

On Saturday, December 15, the *Seattle Times* ran an article with a headline that said, "Isilon Systems takes off in first trading day":

Isilon Systems skyrocketed in its stock market debut Friday, with shares rising 77 percent in the best opening performance for a technology IPO in more than six years.

The Seattle digital storage company took off with a bang from the moment it started trading, with an opening price of $25 per share. It peaked at $27.45—more than double the $13 offering price—before settling down around $23 per share for most of the day. It closed at $23.10, giving the money-losing company a market value of $1.4 billion. . . .

The sharp rise in the stock even surprised some of the Isilon executives, who had gathered on the New York trading floor of Morgan Stanley, the company's principle underwriter. As the "ISLN" ticker symbol flickered across the electronic monitor, Isilon's senior director of marketing, Jay Wampold, said, it "caused us to raise some eyebrows."

"There was a lot of interest and a lot of demand from Wall Street, and I guess that played out today," said Wampold, who was calling from a flight between New York and Seattle.

Wampold, along with Chief Executive Steve Goldman, Chief Financial Officer Stu Fuhlendorf, and Vice President of Marketing Brett Goodwin, were attempting to get back to Seattle to share the news with staffers. They plan to gather tonight in a downtown restaurant. . . .

Isilon's 77 percent gain was the biggest one day "pop" since Santa Clara, Calif.-based chip maker Transmeta posted a 115 percent gain in November 2000.

Shifting Priorities

Monday morning, December 18, I returned to my corner office with the breathtaking view of Puget Sound and the whales playing below. The office buzzed about the *Seattle Times* article and the success of the IPO. Still, I couldn't shake that melancholy feeling. Walking around the office, talking to people, I remember thinking "Is this where I'm going to be for the rest of my career—a public company CFO?" I felt a bit guilty and was rationalizing why I should feel better. "Do you know how many people would give their left arm to be in my situation? It was the product of a lifetime of hard work and self-sufficiency."

Part of my dissatisfaction stemmed from the difficulty of reconciling two significant changes: my sudden wealth and my newfound faith in Christ. All my life, I pursued what was best for myself, depending on my self-sufficiency. I didn't want to rely on anyone. Surrendering my will was unfamiliar ground. I had just heard at church the Sunday after the IPO that the purpose of man is to glorify God and enjoy him forever. Was that my purpose—financially, emotionally, and spiritually? I was already questioning if this was truly my purpose as a new Christian. Now that I had achieved my goals, I realized my wealth could become golden handcuffs, making me dependent on my money, my stock options, my career, my*self*. I wanted to grow in my faith but realized these things could get in the way of growing in dependence on *Christ*.

From that time forward, my love for the Lord flourished, but my life didn't get easier—it got harder as my newfound desires seemed to conflict with the things of the world. Losing the determination to work sixty to eighty hours a week, I pared down my hours to between forty and fifty. With the extra time, I read books. My ravenous appetite for spiritual food drove me to read fifty Christian books that first year. I also regularly attended our church community group, plugged into more of the church ministries, and tried to spend more time with my wife and family.

Trish could tell a change was happening inside me, but I didn't talk about my London experience with her for a few years. I found myself still struggling with my own sins, often at a deep and profound level. I was learning about the gospel of Jesus Christ and his grace—yet I still battled my lingering issues. Believe it or not, my internal struggle with putting off my old self and putting on Christ was so difficult I turned to my prior comforter: alcohol. My drinking actually increased after coming to faith due to this internal conflict.

You could call it growing pains of a young believer. My first few years as a follower of Christ were difficult because as I grew in my relationship with God, I also became increasingly aware of my sinfulness and how to handle it. Trish could see me changing and at times would put her arms around me saying, "I'm worried about how you are struggling." The fire of God was definitely purifying the gold of a new Christian man in his early forties.

While my life began changing, so did my situation at Isilon. As my priorities shifted, I could no longer make Isilon the primary focus of my life. My coworkers could tell that I no longer had the desire and intensity to engage with the same degree of attention to the details. Consequently, leading up to the IPO and unaware to me, a few of our salespeople negotiated unwritten side agreements with certain customers that would result in future problems with the company's financial statements. For example, a few of our early customers received our cutting-edge technology with verbal guarantees from salespeople that the product could be returned at some unknown point in the future. These deals are known as contingent sales. If this was the case it would mean that sales revenue couldn't be recognized for those deals until the customers accepted the product with no right to return it.

As the CFO, I was responsible for overseeing the finances, but the discussions occurred apart from me. Board members, auditors, PriceWaterhouseCoopers and others researched the problem, but no one ever asked me about these deals—not once. Not that I was an accounting expert (I wasn't), but even many months after the troubling problems came to light, no one asked me about what I knew or what I had done. If they had, they would learn that I wasn't involved in or aware of any side deals or subsequent accounting irregularities.

The bigger issue for me was that I was clearly going from being an insider and part of the solution to being an outsider and part of the problem. I was still a team player, but I could no longer pledge allegiance to Isilon above my family and my faith. Part of the reason for this change was my growing faith. I was learning from spiritual giants like St. Augustine that "Pride is the pregnant mother that gives birth to all sin." Another reason I was becoming more detached from Isilon was company politics and the ambition of some people to gain greater control in the company. The behavior and ambition of some within the company created great consternation and stress for me and was painfully damaging my reputation.

Separation and New Direction

In late summer of 2007, some board members asked me to collect some documentation on certain deals and technology. (I wasn't a technologist.) After collecting the data, I walked into a conference room to present my findings to a couple of board members. They were on a conference call. They stopped talking once I entered the room and asked me to leave. I sensed that something was going on, but I wasn't aware of the specific issue. At that moment it became very clear that I needed to think about protecting myself legally.

I called Craig Sherman, the outside general counsel for Isilon, and asked him for a reference for the best litigation lawyer he knew, in case the board members accused me of anything. I wasn't worried about being fired as much as I was concerned that I was being set up as a scapegoat for some shenanigans that I didn't know about. Craig gave me Peter Ehrlichman's name and said that Peter was the best litigator he knew. I didn't know Peter at the time, but I later learned that his dad, John Ehrlichman, served in President Nixon's administration and was a key figure in the Watergate scandal. As you will learn, Peter and his legal partner at the time, Curt Hineline, later became very important people in my life.

Peter agreed to represent me if needed, and it was comforting to know that the D&O (directors and officers) liability insurance of Isilon would likely pay for his services. He provided wise counsel as the behind-the-scenes discussions continued—and it became clear that something was up without my knowledge. I knew my days at Isilon were numbered.

I felt comforted during those times of uncertainty by knowing that God was in control of all of this. On Sunday mornings, I learned that if I became too dependent on worldly positions and possessions, God would orchestrate situations in my life to make me less dependent on them, for his glory and my good. Good things that become God things (or take the place of God) become bad things. Over the years, I accumulated many good things that had become God things. In Acts 9, I read about the apostle Paul's conversion on the road to Damascus. God blinded

Paul for a time for his glory and Paul's good. While I was no apostle Paul, I sensed God leading me through my crisis just like he did with Paul.

On a quiet evening in October 2007 I sat in my office working. All of my reports and most of the staff left early when Sujal Patel, the founder of the company, and Keenan Conder, Isilon's new in-house counsel, entered my office. Little did I know that other board members were meeting with Steve Goldman at the same time.

"Stu," Sujal began. "The board has decided to let you go as CFO."

"Okay," I said. "For what reason?"

"That will be coming out in the future, but we're letting you go."

"Okay." (God's will, I thought). "If that's where it's going, then so be it."

The conversation was very short. I collected my personal belongings in a box—a new experience for me—then Keenan walked me to the elevator.

"I'm sorry about this," he said as he gave me a hug. After the IPO I discovered that Keenan loved Jesus and was a devout Christian.

"Hey, God's will," I replied as the elevator doors closed. My time at Isilon was over.

I drove to my son's basketball practice that night and sat outside in the high school parking lot and called Steve Goldman.

"I don't know if you know this," I told him. "But I just got fired."

"The same thing happened to me," he replied.

On Thursday, October 25, 2007, the *Seattle Post* ran an article in their business section with the headline: "Isilon stock falls further after CEO, CFO resign":

> After several disappointing quarters as a public company, the chief executive and chief financial officer of Isilon Systems have stepped down in a management shake-up that sent the struggling digital storage company's stock down nearly 6 percent Wednesday.
> Sujal Patel, who founded the Seattle company seven years ago and served as its chief technology officer, has assumed the CEO role. He replaces the former F5 Networks executive who joined Isilon in 2003.
>
> Chief Financial Officer Stu Fuhlendorf also has left the company, replaced on an interim basis by controller Bill Richter.

The fact that the company told the Post I had "resigned" was one of many "misrepresentations" that would be portrayed about me in days and years to come. However, I had reached a point in my life where I recognized a glorious God was breaking down my destructive pride. He was nurturing my humility and breaking down my pride—whether I liked it or not.

EIGHT

BAPTISM
BY WATER AND FIRE

Getting fired from a high-profile job—especially in light of our successful IPO—was a blow to my ego. In the days that followed, I feared that I would never get a good job again because of the damage to my reputation. I wasn't accustomed to failing, and this was a big failure.

Initially, the news stunned me, and I felt nothing. But as the shock wore off, a paralyzing cloud of depression haunted me. I still believed deeply that Isilon Systems would be a raving success. The business stood on solid footing and was positioned to grow like a weed as the need for digital content storage was accelerating in the market. I felt angry about missing out on the ride, and I was also in the dark about what I would do next.

To the best of my ability, I tried to stay busy, but the blow to my ego kept reminding me of my "failure." My mind just couldn't comprehend how I could be dismissed.

The only coping mechanism I knew to dull the pain was drinking. The bottle was my closest companion during times of joy and anguish—and everything in between. Alcohol was my functional god before I became a Christian, and it continued as my functional god even after encountering the *real* God who loved me. I drank more and more in the evenings. On really bad days if I didn't have much to do, I started at noon.

In retrospect, seeking God and his will regarding my future would have been extremely beneficial, but as a young Christian, I spent more time thinking about my next steps while medicating my fears with alcohol. I didn't seek counseling or mentoring from godly men, who were becoming increasingly prevalent in my life. I still made decisions based on my views and opinions. *Self-sufficiency.*

The previous year, I had purchased a two-acre property in the west Seattle suburb of Woodway that bordered Puget Sound. The view of Puget Sound was magnificent, and the surrounding neighborhood was one of the wealthiest and trendiest in the Pacific Northwest. Because my net worth was still tied up in Isilon stock options, we had little liquidity. So, I purchased the Woodway property with bank debt. I borrowed $900,000 and purchased the property while Trish was visiting her family in Colorado. I informed her of the transaction during a phone conversation and could tell it bothered her that I would make such a big decision without her— but it didn't surprise her. Then, over the next few months,

before my termination, I hired an architect to design an
eight-thousand-square foot Mediterranean villa that I now
realize was nothing more than a temple to *me*. That was
my modus operandi at various times in our marriage. I
didn't need advice from anyone, including her, and I
would make decisions based on my opinions without
guidance from others. *Self-sufficiency.*

According to the conditions of my Isilon stock option
agreement, upon my termination, I had six months to cash
out my stock options. To my dismay, stock prices spiraled
more than 75 percent from the initial public offering after
news broke of Steve Goldman's and my firing.

Heading into 2008, we stopped construction
on the house and immediately placed the property on
the market. Given the state of the market at the time, I
assumed it would sell quickly. It didn't. The market for
raw, undeveloped property was slowing down rapidly in a
market on the verge of collapse—though no one knew it at
the time. I then made plans to cash out my $1.8 million of
stock options to generate cash flow and purchase another
business. Remember that when the stock went public, it
was valued at nearly $10 million.

With stock prices down and investors feeling
edgy, the board decided to clean house in 2008. By the
end of the year, many of my colleagues on the executive
team were gone, including Brett Goodwin, John Briant,
and other members from the original Isilon executive
team.

I approached my old friend John Briant, whom I dearly trusted, to see if he would be interested in going into business together. We could pool our existing assets and stock options to purchase a business in the Pacific Northwest. So we met at the Snoqualmie Country Club and put together a strategic business acquisition plan, outlining a mutual vision and mission that would help us determine our next venture. We considered start-up tech companies, appliance businesses, art studios, manufacturing services, and many other businesses in various industries.

Isilon Wasn't Finished with Me

Peter Ehrlichman and Kurt Hineline (my other co-lead lawyer) informed me that Isilon was assessing their 2004 through 2007 financial statements, evaluating their various deals and deciding whether to try collecting payments from some customers that were long overdue or relieving them of their payment obligations. If they took the steps of relieving the customers from overdue payments, they would choose to restate their financials, which is a *big* deal for a public company.

Restating financials carries significant legal ramifications for CFOs. After the Sarbanes-Oxley Act of 2002, CEOs and CFOs signed quarterly financial statements, making them personally liable. In other words, if there was an air of any financial impropriety during my tenure as CFO, whether I was directly involved or knew nothing about it, I could be held personally liable in a civil, or worse, a criminal lawsuit.

Isilon was making decisions *after* my termination that directly affected me, and I could do nothing about it nor say anything to them. I felt very much out of control and knew I was at risk, depending on the direction the company would go with their prior financial statements. But I was confident, based on what I knew, that the deals at Isilon up to the IPO were conducted with good intent and with proper accounting. Based on my knowledge of revenue recognition, but more importantly based on the expertise of the CPAs who worked at the firm and the external auditor, the deals recognized revenues appropriately according to FASB (Financial Account Standards Board), and GAAP (Generally Accepted Accounting Principles). Nevertheless, rumors about Steve Goldman and me bounced around the business community like a ball in a pachinko game. My first time dealing with a public failure. At least Isilon's D&O insurance would pay all my legal fees if the company restated financials and I got sued.

The pressure from all of this found its way to my relationship with Trish. She could see the toll this turmoil was taking on me, but I was ill-equipped to cope. At times I felt so overwhelmed with despair that I considered committing suicide.

One evening, after drinking too much, I sat on the edge of the bed and wept.

"Stu," Trish said as she wrapped her arms around me. "I'm concerned that unless you give this situation to God and trust him to deal with it, you're going to die from the stress."

"Good," I replied. That evening, death seemed like a viable alternative.

As time passed, we attended worship together and I continued reading my Bible and devotionals and theological books to feed my young faith. In addition to the Bible, books like *The Man in the Mirror* by Patrick Morley and *Stronger* by Brian "Head" Welch (the ex-guitarist for Korn) brought me great comfort. But I still didn't tell Trish about my experience in England. I felt moments of great joy about Jesus saving me, but I still battled the sins of my past: drinking, gambling, anger, and pride.

After committing my life to Jesus Christ, my conscience came alive—for good and for bad. As I assessed my life before Christ, I was wracked with guilt. How could God ever forgive an underserving sinner like me? But asking a question like that only revealed the depths of my pride. Did I really believe I could commit a sin too great for God to forgive?

Reading the stories in the Bible, I noticed evidence of God's grace and mercy on people as undeserving of me.

Moses witnessed someone abusing one of his people and felt that it was his role to stick up for them. Out of anger and pride, he killed that man (Exodus 2:11-12).

True enough, murder was not a rational response. Yet God used Moses to deliver Israel from slavery to the Egyptians and lead them into the promised land.

The Bible tells us King David was a man after God's own heart (1 Samuel 13:14). He also committed adultery with another man's wife, impregnated her, and then abused his power by having the woman's husband murdered (2 Samuel 11). Nevertheless, God blessed this man who is considered Israel's greatest king.

Before his conversion, Saul (whom we know as the apostle Paul), took pleasure in the murder of Christians. Yet God still called him to follow Christ and transformed him into the greatest Christian missionary in world history.

It became clear to me that I was no better, or worse, than these men. And if these men could be the recipients of God's underserving grace, then maybe I could receive the same.

A Life Changing Investment Before the Storm

Eventually, I found what seemed like a viable business with decent cash flow that interested me. As a result of my heavy drinking, I had developed a palate for wine. In my research, I found a wine distributorship for sale in Portland.

Domaine Selections distributed high-end international wines to the Oregon market. The owner was a Greek immigrant who had built the business over many years with about 1,250 different wines from around the world, which they sold in grocery stores and restaurants. The profits were strong enough to generate an attractive return on investment and enabled him to pay for his kids' college. As long as the economy stayed strong, it was a solid cash-flow business.

I presented the opportunity to John, who looked at the numbers. Although located in Oregon instead of Washington, it was only a three-hour drive away, and we speculated that down the road we could possibly expand the business into Washington.

At the time, John was dealing with some difficult family matters. His lovely daughter, Mackenzie— "Mackey"—was born with a heart defect and underwent a heart transplant at an early age. Due to complications resulting from the improper administration of medicine by paramedics during a health crisis the prior year, her heart stopped. Paramedics resuscitated her, but she sustained severe brain damage. Mackey needed care twenty-four hours a day and was constantly at risk of her body rejecting her heart. Needless to say, like me, John felt some pressure to move into a business that generated significant cash flow. After we visited the business, we agreed to make an offer for Domaine Selections, which the owner accepted.

John and I cashed in our stock options, I paid off some personal debts, and we purchased one of the leading wine distributorships in the state of Oregon.

We drove back and forth from Seattle for a while before renting a townhome in the trendy Northeast area of Portland. We installed a new information technology system to track inventory and modernize accounting and hired a secretary. Confident about the potential to grow, John and I applied for a $200,000 loan to purchase the Henry Wine Group, another wine distribution operation in the Pacific Northwest.

For the first year the business flourished.

In September of 2008, I flew to Las Vegas to meet some friends for a weekend of drinking and gambling. As a young Christian, I knew that my addictions were out of control, but I tried to ignore the lingering guilt inside. Monday night, September 29, I sat at a blackjack table with my friends in the Venetian with a $30,000 line of credit at my disposal. While we were having a good time, a news report on a nearby TV announced that the stock market had collapsed. Some of my friends at the table worked on Wall Street, and I could see the panic in their eyes.

"The world as we know it is coming to an end," one of my investment banking friends stammered in between frantic calls on his cell phone while standing at the blackjack table. "Markets are collapsing, and there are Wall Street firms that aren't going to make it. The whole financial system is going to collapse."

"Dude," I said. "These cycles come and go. This is just a buying opportunity."

"You don't get it," he replied as the volume of his voice started to climb. "It's different this time. The whole system has been rigged, and it's getting ready to collapse."

I just laughed at him.

Pointing his middle finger at me, he yelled, "F*** you!"

Undeterred, I flew home resolving to make Domaine Selections work.

Any business person worth their salt knows that discretionary spending disappears during an economic collapse—and the Great Recession of 2008 was no different. As discretionary income plummeted, so did our wine revenues.

Nevertheless, John and I sought to move forward with due haste and build the business. John generally took a more conservative approach to business while I was the risk-taker. Though we had some difficult discussions, we decided to move forward with our plans. Who knew whether this would be a minor market correction or if we were headed into another depression like October 1929? We decided to follow through on purchasing the Henry Wine Group, signing personally for the bank loan, which would also enable us to invest more money in the business and expand into Washington.

Looking back, I readily acknowledge that we significantly underestimated the extent and impact of the Great Recession. In my arrogance, I believed that John and I could outsmart our competition and prove to the bankers—and anyone else who cared—that we could make it work . . . regardless of the market conditions.

As the economy struggled, consumers stopped spending money on luxury items like fine wines, and Domaine Selection revenues decreased. In the face of mounting pressure, John and I buckled down, working harder to grow the business and incurring additional bank debt, again which we signed for personally.

Additionally, my real estate broker informed me that the $900,000 piece of property we purchased in Woodway was now worth half that due to the collapse of the real estate market, so we were underwater on the loan by nearly half a million dollars.

We exhausted all of our reserves and were quickly running out of cash.

The Pressure Grew on All Fronts

Meanwhile, pressures concerning Isilon continued to mount. Peter Ehrlichman told me Isilon was thinking of restating their financials, and if they did, the SEC might come after me. He didn't know whether it would be a civil or criminal case, but it would happen in the next year. The worst-case scenario, if I lost, I would have to serve time in jail.

Waiting for bad news seems to slow down the clock and speed up the rapid-fire thoughts in my brain. Finally, Peter called me with an update.

"Stu, Isilon has decided to restate some of their financial statements between 2004 and 2007, regardless of the risk it places on you. They told me that it's in the best interest of their existing customers, and they truly believe that the accounting treatment was incorrect, given the structure of some of the deals."

I didn't know how to reply because I was in shock.

"This is bad for you," he continued. "They know it, and it's very clear after talking with them that they are willing to throw you under the bus. So get ready for a long battle, depending on how the SEC responds to the restatement."

"Okay," I finally mumbled. "Thanks for the info." What else could I say? I had no control over the situation.

It felt like someone shut off the spigot of hope. My reputation was destroyed and any dream of returning to the corporate world was gone. Frankly, after my conversion in London, I wasn't sure God wanted me in the corporate world anyway.

And how did I respond to the stress of a struggling business in a collapsed economy and a potential lawsuit from the Securities Exchange Commission? I drank and spent long hours and many days working at Domaine Selections.

Part of my job as an owner of a wine distribution business was to sample the various wines we carried and taste new wines at wine shows. Professionals normally spit out the wines they taste, but not me. I started "sampling" our wines early in the mornings, doing whatever I could to alleviate the pressure. As you can guess, my drinking affected my job performance.

Yet as I began surrendering my situation to God, I sensed that he had me right where he wanted me, which brought great comfort. In his sovereign wisdom and will, he baptized me in the raging fire of his love and was using the various problems I was facing for his purpose and my good, faithfully burning my impurities. Privately I cried out to God to deliver me, as King David did in the Psalms, and I found encouragement reading passages like 1 Peter 5:6-11:

> Humble yourselves, therefore, under the mighty hand of God so that at the proper time he may exalt you, casting all your anxieties on him, because he cares for you. Be sober-minded; be watchful. Your adversary the devil prowls around like a roaring lion, seeking someone to devour. Resist him, firm in your faith, knowing that the same kinds of suffering are being experienced by your brotherhood throughout the world. And after you have suffered a little while, the God of all grace, who has called you to his eternal glory in Christ, will himself restore, confirm, strengthen, and establish you. To him be the dominion forever and ever. Amen.

Before becoming a Christian, I would have never gotten a tattoo, but when I read this, I had the Scripture reference tattooed on my left shoulder. It reminds me of who is in control and how God purifies gold with the fire.

John and I pressed our feet on the accelerator and raised more money and brought in two more business partners. It was a disastrous decision due to the volatile market situation, and the personalities of the two people didn't mesh with John and me.

We hoped the economy would recover faster, but it didn't.

That March, I returned to Las Vegas—much to the chagrin of Trish— to join some old high school and Wall Street buddies for a weekend of drinking, gambling, and watching the first weekend of March Madness (the NCAA basketball tournament). We rented a suite in the Venetian and started partying, betting on basketball games and playing craps. Saturday night, after drinking nonstop since Thursday, my friends, Jim and Kevin, and I decided to eat sushi across the street at the Bellagio.

A group of military men and their wives or girlfriends sat at a table near ours. In my altered state, I approached their table, thanked them for their service, and offered to buy them a bottle of Dom Perignon champagne.

When I returned to my table, Kevin and I got into a political discussion about the US military that escalated into an argument. Kevin's dad had served in the military, and he felt our wars overseas were a travesty. I disagreed with him. Lubricated by three days of drinking, our debate quickly intensified.

I'm sure that in a sober state of mind, the argument would have taken a different tone than it did, but it became personal.

At one point, I stood up, grabbed a cup of beer, threw it in his face, and marched out of the restaurant. After walking out the door and turning the corner, I decided that the fight wasn't over. So I walked back into the restaurant, glared at him, picked up another beer, threw it in his face again, and walked off.

Back in my hotel room at the Venetian, as I started sobering up, I realized the utter depravity of my actions. I crawled into bed and woke up the next morning feeling hungover and ashamed. Instead of talking to my friends, I packed my bags and hopped on an earlier flight to Seattle.

My actions that night destroyed my friendship with Kevin. To this day, our relationship has not been reconciled, though I pray for him often and truly love my old friend. The financial stress, my termination from Isilon, a potential lawsuit from the SEC, and my drinking culminated in a perfect storm that I regret to this day. I repented of my behavior toward Kevin, and though God is gracious, some sins wreak havoc for a lifetime. King David is my example. He was a man after God's heart, but he suffered the consequences of certain sins his entire life.

One of God's blessings from the carnage of that night, is that it brought clarity to the disparity between my faith and my actions. Never before had I seen my sins so magnified. I was mortified and knew I needed an internal and external alignment. My drinking needed to stop, and I needed to lose weight. Most important, I decided to go all-in with my relationship with Jesus Christ. I remember sitting in church the next Sunday and feeling very strongly that it was time to get baptized. I loved Jesus, and it was time to make a public confession. I decided to get baptized on Easter Sunday 2009.

My Baptism Was the Fulfillment of a Dream

The Saturday night before the big day, I went to bed, not really thinking about baptism or anything in particular. While asleep, I experienced the most realistic dream of my life. About three o'clock in the morning, I awoke and sat up in bed.

"Trish, wake up. I need to tell you something."

"Can it wait 'til morning?"

"No! You need to hear this!"

"Okay," she murmured. "Go ahead."

"Trish, I dreamed that I was at my funeral. I was floating above the casket, and I could see myself. John Briant gave the eulogy and at the end, a man holding a set of bagpipes walked down the aisle playing 'Amazing Grace.' It was so real, Trish."

"Okay. Did anything else happen?"

"No, that was it."

"You woke me up to tell me that?"

"Yeah," I chuckled. "You're right. Let's go back to sleep."

The next day my father and his significant other, Pattie, showed up at Mars Hill Church, along with Trish, Erich, and Hannah. Then to my surprise, John Briant, his wife, Elaine, and their children, Ethan and Mackey, came in. Navigating the crowd with Mackey's wheelchair was a production, but despite the challenges, they proceeded with smiles on their faces.

Mars Hill Church was a rock-and-roll kind of church. They played worship songs, many of them based on hymns but with a grungy Seattle sound. After the singing, Mark Driscoll preached about baptism, and then the baptisms began. I was the first of approximately twenty people to get baptized. The moment I stepped into the baptism tank, I felt overwhelmed with a sense of joy and a connection to Jesus that I had never experienced before. I was floating on air.

An associate pastor and his wife stood with me in the tank and asked me if I had accepted Jesus Christ as my Lord and Savior. I said yes, and they immersed me in front of a couple thousand people.

I came out of the water feeling like a new person with many of the pressures of my prior life washed away. It felt like a burden was lifted from my shoulders.

As I stepped out of the baptismal, Trish held me in her arms. She didn't care that I was wet. With tears streaming down her face, she said, "This is a big day!"

"Honey, to God be the glory," I replied.

Then she returned to her seat in the sanctuary, and I walked into a back room where I was interviewed on video camera for the rest of the church to see.

"What led you to this point?" the interviewer asked me.

"God's sovereignty," I answered. "His elective grace alone. I climbed the corporate ladder and reached the top only to discover that it was empty. Then I fell off the ladder and my life right now is really hard. But praise God, I have my wife and my family, and God is going to see us through it."

My heart felt like it was about to burst with joy, much like that night when I gave my life to Christ in London.

After the baptisms and Easter Service concluded, a side door to the auditorium opened, and in walked a man dressed in a kilt, strolling down the aisle playing "Amazing Grace."

The song sounded very familiar. Then, when I remembered my dream from earlier that morning, I looked down the row of people where Trish sat, our family members sitting between us. She was bending over, looking at me with tears streaming down her face. We both knew that God was at work in my life.

Afterward, Trish and I held each other a for a long time.

"Why are you guys so emotional?"

We looked over to see my daughter, Hannah. Then we told her the story about my dream of the bagpipe player at my funeral.

"Of course," she said. "The baptism symbolized dying to yourself, just like a funeral. And then you came up out of the water and all of your sins were washed clean, like a new man."

Pretty insightful for a junior in high school!

Not lost was the fact that John Briant appeared in my dream and showed up unexpectedly at my baptism.

It had been two and a half years since I yielded my life to Christ at the Savoy Hotel.

After getting fired from Isilon, making some dumb financial decisions, ruining a relationship with a dear friend, seeing my drinking problem grow, struggling with my flesh, and realizing the depths of my sin, God still providentially put me in a position to confess my faith in him and to be baptized on that Easter Sunday.

You would think that my life would get easier, but it didn't. It got harder. Much harder.

NINE

SINK AND SWIM

"**S**tu, I just looked at the January sales figures, and it doesn't look good."

John and I were talking business in our Portland warehouse.

"That's no surprise," I answered. "But if we just stick with it until the economy turns around, this will all be worth it. The problem is we don't know when it *is* going to turn around. This is as bad as I've seen the economy."

My business partner agreed. "Until we can recover from this recession, the discretionary income for the upper-end wines just won't be there."

"John, we're in a tough spot, and the way I see it, there are a couple ways we can work our way through this. We can either tighten our belts and fight through this or we can step on the accelerator with more wines and salespeople. We've already committed to the purchase of Henry Wine Group and we're expanding into Washington during a tough time. We may have already bitten off more than we can chew given the uncertainty in the market."

"I agree," John said. "We're in a tough spot and we've already made commitments. We always keep commitments, but it's going to be a struggle for a long while."

As much as we wanted the economy to pull out of its tailspin, the annual forecast in early 2009 didn't look positive. At Domaine Selections, John and I were doing our best to keep our heads above water. If any two business executives could make this work, it was us.

It wasn't working.

To make matters worse, after purchasing our company we discovered that Domaine Selections suffered from internal problems that hadn't been disclosed to us. Within the first year, key suppliers were going to our competitors. We were working through the lingering effects of disclosure issues, so I was renegotiating the purchase price with the original owner by lowering the purchase note that he was carrying. He had agreed to the terms, but it didn't make the situation any easier given the state of the economy.

John and I steeled our resolve to make Domaine Selections work. We continued moving forward on purchasing the Henry Wine Group and bringing more product on board. To house the increased inventory, we moved out of our old, rustic warehouse and into a renovated warehouse in Northeast Portland. Then we focused on expanding our operations into the state of Washington. Remember, we were new to the wine business. I knew how to build a technology company and take a company public, but that was nothing like building a wine business . . . in the midst of a struggling economy when similar businesses were dropping like flies.

So John and I focused our energies trying to repair and grow the company during a distressing season. At the same time, John continued to deal with significant family issues surrounding the health of Mackey.

Like John, I also dealt with other significant issues. I knew that financing our company with personal debt was risky, but my determination to succeed overruled my common sense. Fortunately, I was able to keep Trish's name off any of the documents. The bank through whom I borrowed money to purchase our personal property and build an edifice to me in Edmonds was pressuring me to refinance given my departure from Isilon Systems. I had borrowed the money as unsecured debt, without offering any collateral and they had accepted the terms. But I was willing to sign the property over as collateral in case of default. They reluctantly agreed because they had no other choice. I was so underwater on the loan that placing the real estate back on the market would have been disastrous to our finances, and the bank would have taken a bath worth many hundreds of thousands of dollars. I was drowning in debt—both personally and corporately—with little hope on the horizon for recovering.

From Bad ...

In the middle of 2009, Peter Ehrlichman called me with a message I didn't want to hear.

"Stu, I have bad news for you."

"What is it?"

"Isilon has decided to restate their earnings for certain quarters from 2004 through 2007. As you know, you're at personal legal risk. Because you signed the quarterly 10Q and annual 10K earnings statements as the chief financial officer, you may be held personally liable by the Securities and Exchange Commission for the inaccurate statements. If they contend that you purposefully misled or were fraudulent in your intent, they may come after you criminally. No one knows what will happen after the restatement. We need to prepare for possible litigation from the SEC."

"Peter," I exclaimed. "This is complete b******t! Isilon's more intent on placating customers and building the business than doing what's right and working through payment issues with the customers on legacy products. If they really wanted to do what was right, someone should talk to me about the deals. I am beyond perplexed how they can restate earnings and not one member of the board of directors, current executives, external auditors, corporate lawyers, or anyone else representing Isilon has contacted me about any of this over the last couple of years.

"What's the worst-case scenario, Peter?"

"Do you really want to know?"

"I can handle it, Peter. Spit it out."

"If the government comes after you on criminal charges, you could go to jail for years. If they come after you on civil charges, they will come after any net worth you've accumulated over your career. We just don't know what the SEC is going to do, or if they'll even come after you."

"Okay, Peter. Got it, thanks. We'll take care of this and handle it regardless of the outcome. Gotta run."

But I couldn't handle it.

Those nights in Portland, 180 miles away from family, I felt very alone. I cried out to God to rescue me. "Just put me out of my misery," I prayed. "Give me a heart attack. Something!"

Yet, at the same time, I sensed God's mysterious presence in the midst of my suffering. My reputation was being destroyed. My money was being depleted. I was running a business that I didn't know well, and frankly didn't like all that much. The Bible assured me that God loved me and was working all things out for his purpose and my good because I loved him.

But how was any of this working out for my good?

To deal with the stress, I visited our customers' restaurants. I ate their meals and drank copious amounts of wine and cocktails and then returned to the townhouse for more drinking. Other nights I hung out with other people in the wine business or employees for a night of intoxication. Some nights I drank alone.

I drank myself to sleep, only to awaken in the middle of the night, half-sober and overwhelmed with anxiety. The adrenaline from the stress kept me awake during the day until I repeated the same desperate routine the next night. Many evenings, I drank to the point that I passed out.

One morning, while I was back in Seattle for the weekend and recovering from a hangover, Trish sat with me on the edge of my bed, placed her arm around my shoulders, and said, "This is going to kill you if you keep doing this."

"Good," I cried. "It's better than the alternative."

My world was collapsing on me, and I could do nothing to prevent it. No matter how hard we worked to decrease our expenses and increase our sales, Domaine Selections was failing, and I was teetering on the verge of bankruptcy. We were underwater on our Woodway property by a half million dollars, thanks to a stubborn US economy that refused to recover after a massive economic collapse. To top it off, at any moment I knew my lawyers could call me to say the Securities Exchange Commission was suing me and I might serve time in jail.

"If that happens," I fantasized, "I'll make my final exit. The insurance money will take care of Trish and the kids. Then she'll find someone else who won't put her through this hell."

In those dark moments, I considered various scenarios of what my final exit might look like. Driving off a cliff.

Drinking myself to death. Sticking a sharp knife in my abdomen, performing *hara-kiri*, while someone chopped off my head in an honorable general's death. Even though I fantasized about killing myself to make it all go away, deep down I knew suicide was the coward's way out. I felt there was something greater, something more purposeful going on. I could sense it amidst the suffering. Trish was feeling the pain as well, but the issues were so intense that I felt alone on a deserted island.

My life felt like a whack-a-mole game at the county fair, where a mole's head pops up on the table. Someone hits it and then another mole's head appears and gets hit again. I was being pummeled on every side and didn't know if and when it would stop.

Through all of this, Trish continued to love and encourage me, though she was feeling her own pain and insecurities. At times, when I was overwhelmed with depression, Trish would wrap her arms around me and reassure me.

"You're going to be okay. We're going to be okay. God is in control. Just keep digging into God's word."

My men's Bible study also provided me with a lifeline and Alan Artman became a trusted confidante. As I suffered on multiple fronts, Alan confided in me about personal issues in his life and then together we reflected on them from a biblical perspective. Every conversation with him brought me comfort and a peace beyond comprehension.

In my heart of hearts, I knew I was innocent of the allegations, and I hoped that common sense would prevail. At the same time, as I read the Bible, I wondered what being innocent really meant. Fairness began taking on a new meaning to me. I read that while I was a sinner, Christ died for me. How fair was that? Was Jesus treated fairly? My relatively new faith was the result of God's grace and mercy—and I had nothing to do with it. Was that fair?

While pondering these experiences and reflections, I knew other people at Isilon were scurrying around, trying to cover their backsides. Since I no longer worked at Isilon, I was an easy target.

... to Worse

On Friday, September 11, 2009, Peter Ehrlichman and Kurt Hineline called me to say that in three days the SEC was going to file charges against me for accounting and securities fraud. In addition, a story about me was going to appear on the front page of the *Seattle Times* business section. They were going to report that the SEC was implicating me—and me alone—and it wasn't going to be a pretty picture.

In essence, the SEC was accusing me of being a crook. My mind raced. If I lost the case, I would be among the pantheon of criminal business people like Charles Ponzi (known for the Ponzi Scheme), Jeff Skilling and Ken Lay (Enron), and Dennis Koslowski (Tyco).

Peter and Kurt were preparing to drive to Portland when they called. They knew I was a heavy drinker and that I had been struggling on many fronts. Over the prior couple of years, they showed they cared about me more than just as a client. Even without their news, I was teetering on a nervous breakdown, so they wanted to prevent me from making any fatal decisions. That's why they wanted to be with me during this acute crisis.

Nevertheless, I insisted I wouldn't see them.

"Don't waste your time driving all the way to Portland," I thought. "I don't know what I'm going to do, but I don't want anybody around." At that point I wasn't really sure what I was going to do, but I knew I wasn't in the mood to be around anybody.

"Guys," I said, "You can come here if you want, but wild horses aren't going to drag me away to spend time with you. I appreciate the gesture though."

"Okay, Stu" Peter said. "Just know that we're here for you and we're available to talk any time."

"Yeah, okay, Peter," I smirked privately as I thought about where I was going to head for some relief.

I wanted to drown myself in a few Tanqueray on the rocks to numb the pain.

I walked back into the warehouse where John was working on inventory and logistics for the daily deliveries and product orders. We often took turns working in Portland, but that week we both were there.

"John, I just got a phone call from Peter Ehrlichman. I need to get away and think about our conversation, so I'm going to head back to the town house."

"You got it, Stu."

A Life-Changing Call Straight from God

On my way to the town house, thoughts were racing through my head. Securities fraud. Bankruptcy. Jail time. Divorce. Homelessness. Failure. I couldn't stop my fears from spinning out of control. Every scenario for pulling out of my downward spiral seemed hopeless. The anxiety threw me into an adrenaline stupor, giving me a head start on my impending cocktail. After a few drinks, I wasn't sure what I would do with or to myself.

Throughout my life I willingly stepped up and admitted fault for my transgressions. But this time, I knew I was innocent. Granted, I made mistakes in the process, and my newfound faith in Christ divorced me from my marriage to my job, but I never willfully defrauded the company or investors.

Right after entering my Nob Hill apartment, my phone rang. It was a non-descript number. Initially, I assumed it might be a reporter, but I didn't want to take any chance that the caller could also be Peter or Kurt. When the person on the other line announced he was Charles Colson, I refused to believe it. "Really?!" I snorted. "Pull this leg, and it'll play 'Jingle Bells.'"

After a brief awkward silence, the voice on the other side began to laugh. That's when I recognized his voice from listening to him on the radio. It really was *the* Charles Colson.

"A friend of yours gave me your number and asked me to call you," he began. "I understand you're being sued by the SEC. I can imagine the press is going to be all over your story."

"Yeah, Chuck," I replied. "But you need to know that I'm innocent. I didn't do anything wrong."

My pride and need to defend myself was already apparent.

Then he chuckled again. "Oh really? Well, I *did* do it." I knew from reading *Born Again* that he was referring to his involvement in Watergate, which resulted in his conviction and jail time.

From reading his books and listening to him on the radio, I knew he understood the depth and pervasiveness of humanity's depravity. He was just trying to let me know that even if I had intentionally committed the crime, he understood and would support me as a Christian brother.

"Stu, I understand your situation, and let me tell you from experience, this isn't going to be easy. It'll likely get worse. During Watergate, I admitted what I did, and the courts threw me in jail. In one sense, I lost everything. But you know what? I gained everything in return.

"Jesus said in Luke 9:24 (NIV), 'whoever wants to save his life will lose it, but whoever loses his life for me

will save it.' I left behind my life of lying, stealing, pride—
and in return I gained my soul.

"And you know what? God is in control. He's
sovereign, so he can do whatever he wants. But, I'm
confident about this: you're going to emerge from this a
better person, a more godly person. God has big plans for
you and he is going to work all of this out for his purpose
and your good."

He mentioned the story of Joseph in the Old
Testament book of Genesis. Joseph was betrayed by his
brothers and sold into slavery. Years later, Joseph grew
to become one of the most powerful leaders in Egypt.
Eventually, through his position, he saved the lives of his
brothers who betrayed him years earlier. When Joseph
reconciled with his brothers, he told them, "You intended
to harm me, but God intended it for good."

"God is intimately involved in your situation," he
told me.

The moment I heard Colson's words, my adrenaline
stopped pumping, my heart stopped racing, my thoughts
slowed down, and I felt the comforting presence of the
Holy Spirit. I hadn't felt like this since my salvation in
London on that day in December 2006.

Twenty minutes later, we said goodbye. After getting
off the phone, a gentle peace surrounded me, like a life
vest keeping me afloat in the deep sea. Then I sat on the
living room couch, reflecting on Colson's words and his
kindness in reaching out to somebody he didn't know. I

still hadn't made myself a drink, and my desire to do so subsided, at least for the moment. I reflected on my faith in Jesus. He suffered betrayal and false accusation, which led him to his death on the cross. Suddenly, I felt a deep connection to Jesus. He understood.

Right then, I heard a knock on the door. When I opened it, Trish stood in front of me with tears in her eyes. We held each other and wept. True to form, I hadn't called her upon getting the news of the lawsuit. Instead, Peter and Kurt called Trish when they heard about the pending SEC charges, and she made the immediate decision to drive to Portland to be with me. They told her that they intended to drive down as well, but Trish was already on her way.

That night I didn't get intoxicated, which made Trish happy because I drank almost every day and still weighed over three hundred pounds. Instead Trish and I went out for dinner and talked.

"I'm fine," I assured her. "Once the SEC lawyers take a closer look at the evidence, they'll drop the case. Take my word for it."

I said what I did to keep Trish from worrying, but I knew it wasn't true. In the coming months, I fully expected to face the greatest challenges of my life: prevailing in an impending court trial, overcoming my growing dependency on alcohol, and navigating my way through our personal financial and business turmoil. But at the same time, I detected a glimmer of hope. Somehow, some way, God was going to rescue this depraved sinner and shine his light in the midst of my darkness.

In just a few days, September 14, 2009, my darkest days were going to provide a great opportunity for the light to shine the brightest.

TEN

BREAKING THROUGH
THE WALL

SEC files charges against Isilon's former finance chief

The Securities and Exchange Commission has charged a former chief financial officer of Isilon with cutting secret side deals that resulted in inflated sales numbers after the Seattle company went public in 2006.

Stuart Fuhlendorf allegedly hid the actual terms of the deals from Isilon's controller, audit committee and auditor, leading the data-storage company to report $4.8 million in improper revenue, the SEC alleges.

"Fuhlendorf did not mislead the company or its shareholders," said Peter Ehrlichman, his attorney at Dorsey & Whitney. "The SEC complaint is a story that will not hang together when the facts come out."

No one can prepare for the public humiliation I suffered when I read the *Seattle Times* article that Tuesday morning in 2009. I didn't sleep well the night before it was released because I didn't know what it would say—and it was worse than I expected. The one-sided condemnation caught me by surprise, but thanks to Peter Ehrlichman, he defended me well. I knew Peter genuinely believed in my case and told me I was innocent of the charges and that Isilon had thrown me under the bus. His support meant the world to me.

Still, I knew that even if Peter persuaded the jury to drop my case, my career as a CFO was likely over. I already came to terms that God was moving me in a different direction, and I felt at peace with the prospect. Even if the charges were resolved in a positive way, I no longer desired a career as a corporate executive.

In light of the allegations, focusing on our failing wine business was difficult. I felt overwhelmed by the implosion in my life and quite often I wondered if we would ever escape the fallout. The wrongful accusations, SEC litigation, trying to keep a struggling business out of bankruptcy, and watching my reputation get pummeled were multiple gut punches to my pride and self-confidence. Restless nights became a constant companion as I tried to imagine a different life. In my young faith, I knew God was at work in the middle of it. I just couldn't tell how. Still, I turned to alcohol to alleviate the stress. My penchant for hard liquor and the easy accessibility to wine provided me an easy escape. The resulting guilt and shame from my drinking binges led to feelings of depression. To push back the despair, I prayed and read my Bible quite often. I really sensed God's presence. But the bottle remained my closest confidante. Instead of welcoming the morning with a cup of coffee, I downed a few glasses of wine before leaving for work. Then I continued my wine "tasting," and imbibed a few martinis with clients or lawyers over lunch before going back to work.

After work, if I was in Seattle, I hit the bars with or without other people. Often when I woke up in the morning, I couldn't remember how I got home. One morning, I woke up and didn't see my car in the garage. My first thought was that my car had been stolen. Later I learned that my car was still parked outside a neighborhood bar. Somebody either drove me home or I walked. I just don't know.

Other days, if I was working in Seattle, I would get home by five or six in the evening and drink so much that I passed out on the couch. Because the couch was in our family room, Trish and Hannah would sit on one end and watch television in the evenings, while I'd be passed out on the other end. In the morning, if there was any vomit in the house from my drinking, I'd clean it up, shower, suck down a glass or two of wine, and leave for work. Then I'd repeat the routine when I returned home.

Some mornings I apologized, usually to Hannah, for something rude I'd said in my drunken stupor and promised to never do it again and get sober. Then I would do it again.

When Things Couldn't Get Worse . . . They Did

To blow off a little steam, I spent one long day at the Muckleshoot Casino guzzling as many gins on the rocks as I could handle. Driving home that night, a police officer pulled me over because I was weaving down the road.

When he told me he was going to give me a breathalyzer test, I told him to go f*** himself, so he handcuffed me and took me to jail. Later that night, Trish and Hannah picked me up and drove me home. Trish was furious beyond belief. She yelled at me all the way home, while Hannah sat in the back seat, incredulous.

Because I refused to breathe into the breathalyzer, I was charged with the most serious DUI offense. For the rest of 2010, I spent thousands of dollars fighting my DUI with the help of my lawyer.

In the midst of the dispute, I remembered reading in *Born Again* how Charles Colson responded to his Watergate allegations. He admitted what he had done.

After thinking and praying, I decided to do the same and take responsibility for my actions. So I met with my lawyer and told him the news.

"Ben," I began. "I've had a change of heart. I want to take responsibility for my actions and plead guilty to the DUI charges."

"Are you kidding me?" he responded. His beet-red face told me he wasn't pleased with my intentions. "We've been working hard on your case. You have a good chance of beating this thing."

"Quit fighting it," I said. "I'm going to plead guilty because I *am* guilty."

Sure enough, the DA threw the book at me. He gave me a full-blown DUI conviction, which required a blower being installed in my vehicle, a $1,500 fine and twenty-four hours in the King County jail.

Trish fully supported me pleading guilty. We both knew the penalty would be harsh, but we also knew that it was the right thing to do. In fact, she was relieved by my confession and understood that my acknowledgement of guilt pointed to my growing faith. Prior to appearing before the judge, we discussed how repentance included contrition, confession, and change. For me, in order to continue to change, I needed to be contrite and willing to confess.

However, my life was an obvious contradiction. It was up and down. I did everything in *my* power to focus on my Christian walk. At times, I could recognize God's sovereign hand in my life because I felt an incomprehensible peace that he was at work in the mess. Yet I struggled to break free from defining myself by my actions and the opinions of others. My career was in shambles, our net worth was plummeting, we were buried under incredible debt due to the land we still owned in Woodway, and the demons of guilt and shame harassed me day and night. One moment I felt God's presence all around me. The next moment I felt very alone and desperate.

I struggled with the idea that God loved me in the midst of the mess I created. Then, I read in the Bible that God's hand was in the mess. For instance, in the book of Exodus, God's people were enslaved by the Egyptians for more than four hundred years, but we know he never abandoned them, nor did he give up on his plan to use them in future generations to save the world through Jesus. His grand plan was always present for his people. I tried to earn God's love, making deals with him to clean up my life if he'd deliver me from the pain.

"If you rescue the business and overturn the lawsuit," I bargained with God, "I'll give you anything . . . everything." But in my heart of hearts, I know if he had answered my request, I still would have held on.

God didn't seem to answer my prayer. I learned later that he *did*, in fact, answer my prayer. His answer was no and for my own good and his purpose. Through my good works I tried to show God that I was worthy of his love. But in reality, I could never do enough to earn his love. No one can.

In retrospect, I can see that I couldn't promise God anything because everything belonged to him anyway. I was clinging to self-sufficiency and didn't want to let go. I was terrified to let go. Everything in my life—my career, my finances, my family, my reputation—was under attack.

I felt despair. Abandoned. Disconnected. Resentful. Suicidal.

In other words, God had me right where he wanted me.

I Finally Hit the Wall

By the middle of 2010, I could see that Domaine Selections wasn't going to pull out of the Great Recession, partly because we were overleveraged from buying the Henry Wine Group. My SEC lawsuit and the repercussions of my DUI distracted me from the business, so I wasn't much help in turning the company around. That left John to work overtime to keep the business afloat while valiantly dealing with issues at home.

In early September, Trish decided to go home to Colorado to visit her mother and siblings. I remained in Seattle to work on the SEC lawsuit and deal with the many issues that plagued our struggling business. Because the kids were away at college, I spent the next week by myself without anyone to monitor my drinking.

In the *Divine Comedy*, Dante wrote, "Midway along the journey of my life I woke to find myself in a dark wood, for I had wandered off from the straight path."

The moment Trish left on Saturday, I entered the "dark wood."

Being alone in my house for the week brought all of my pent-up frustrations and growing dependence on alcohol to the surface. Feelings of anger and betrayal from my former coworkers and the board of directors at Isilon bubbled up. Frustration at not being able to make Domaine Selections work consumed me. I resented losing all of my money in the economic collapse. I regretted my DUI conviction. I needed to escape. I needed relief from the stress.

I hit the wall.

On Monday I turned off my cell phone, drove to the liquor store, and bought multiple bottles of vodka and whiskey. Then I picked up cases of wine from the warehouse. I returned home and drank. I drank away my anger and betrayal, my frustration and resentment. At least I *thought* I was drinking it away. All week long, I drank until I passed out. When I woke up, I drank until I passed out again.

Midday Wednesday, I heard a knock on the front door. I staggered to the door and greeted Todd Tarbert, a dear friend who advised us in acquiring Domaine Selections. He is also a follower of Christ. After welcoming him into the house, he surveyed the scattered bottles, raised his eyebrows, and did his best to hide his surprise.

"Hey, listen Stu, I got a call from your wife today. She said you're not responding to her phone calls."

"Well, my phone was off," I said, doing my best to hide my drunken stupor.

Then he looked around the room again.

"I'm taking you out of here."

"You're not taking me anywhere, Todd. Wild horses couldn't drive me out of here." Ironically, I used the same verbiage when Peter and Kurt told me they were coming to Portland in September 2009.

"Stu, you know that we're more than business partners. You're my brother in Christ. I love you, and I'm concerned about you."

Then he told me about a friend who suffered through some of the same issues as me.

"One of my greatest regrets in life," he said, "is that I didn't do enough to help my friend. I'm not going to let it happen again."

"You know that I love you too," I replied. "But I don't want your help."

"Okay," Todd answered as he shrugged his shoulders. "If this is what it takes to hit rock bottom, I guess that's what you need to do."

Then he left and called Trish. He told her that I was alive but clearly in the midst of a weeklong bender.

For the next two days, I drank like a thirsty man in the desert, making for five days of utter inebriation. When Trish walked into the house that Friday, she looked at all the empty bottles scattered around the house, then sat down next to me and said nothing.

I looked at her and said, "I need to check in to rehab, like yesterday!"

Relieved that I had finally hit the wall, Trish immediately called Lakeside-Milam Recovery Center in Kirkland and told them I needed to check into their facility as soon as possible. They informed her that a bed would be available on Monday. Trish then gathered some clothes, walked me to the car, and drove me to the hospital for a medical evaluation.

An hour later, the doctor entered our room. My hands were already shaking from *delirium tremens* (withdrawal symptoms) because I hadn't had a drink in a couple of hours.

"I just received the results of your blood work," he explained to Trish and me. "Your blood alcohol content was 0.35—not 0.035—0.35. A score of 0.45 is death.

Then the doctor looked me straight in the eyes.

"Stu?"

I nodded my head, still feeling woozy from all the drinking.

"Stu," he continued. "You need to get help. If you don't stop drinking, it will kill you. Soon. Please—if not for you, do it for your wife and kids."

"Yes, sir," I replied.

"We're checking him in to rehab on Monday," Trish explained. "I talked to the people at Lakeside-Milam Recovery Center in Kirkland. That's when the next bed is available."

Then the doctor looked at me and told Trish, "I know that you don't want to hear this, but this is going to be a long weekend for you *and* if Stu tells you he needs a drink, you need to go out and buy him alcohol."

"What?!?" Trish asked.

"That's right," he replied. "Alcoholics can die if left to detox on their own. He *must* detox at Lakeside-Milam where the professionals can provide the necessary drugs to get him through."

In my inebriated state, I knew rehab was my only hope for sobriety. I learned soon thereafter that rehab is a great catalyst, but the real hope for sobriety comes from worshipping the only true God, Jesus Christ. I would soon learn that for me, alcohol was a worship disorder and a false idol that delivered nothing but slavery, not freedom. My life needed to change soon. At this point, I was willing to do anything to get well. Alcohol had completely broken me.

Trish refers to the next two days as "the weekend from hell." I was drunk the entire time and wasn't thinking clearly. In fact, I insisted that I needed to go for a bicycle ride and immediately crashed, trashing my legs and my bike. I was outside my right mind. I went back and forth about going to rehab, droning on and on about it. I wouldn't let Trish out of my sight, following her around like a puppy dog, talking incessant nonsense. Truth be told, my behavior frightened her.

She finally told me that she had to go to the bathroom, then locked herself inside and called my father.

"Elvin, Stu will be checking in to rehab on Monday, but right now, he is a mess and I'm frightened. Can you please come over here and stay with us? I can't do this anymore!"

My dad came right over.

Everybody Hits the Wall

That Monday I checked into Lakeside-Milam, where I stayed for the next twenty-eight days. After a checkup, the medical personnel gave me Librium, so I could detoxify. For the next five days I stayed in the detox center sleeping with occasional visits from counselors and patients who would become my mentors.

After five days, I moved into a room with two other men. One of my roommates was a middle-aged vice president of manufacturing for Boeing. The other was a Native American who was a member of the Muckelshoot tribe. He was in rehab for his tenth time, paid for by his tribe. He called rehab vacation.

I immediately started going to counseling. Some of my sessions took place in groups; other times I met with a counselor by myself. During one of my first group sessions, our counselor, Bob, described a wall that each of us faced—a wall that stood between us and sobriety, our ability to move on in life beyond our addictions.

"Everybody hits the wall," he began. "The wall often occurs around a career and business crisis, resentments and feelings of personal entitlements, and substance abuse, like alcoholism. Please write down your reflections on the wall and tell us about yours tomorrow."

In the next morning's session, Bob looked at me. "Stu," he asked. "Tell us, what does *your* wall look like?"

I looked at everyone and then down at what I had written.

"Well, when I consider my wall, the cinder blocks are large and heavy, and the wall itself is fifteen feet high and six feet thick. The only way to break through the wall is methodically and patiently. The cinder blocks are large and imposing with the weight and density of materials like pride, selfishness, fear, envy, resentment, greed, self-will, guilt, shame, suspicion, gluttony, chemical dependency, and a cacophony of misshaped bricks that were made of sundry sins and worldly pleasures."

I continued, "I am in the process of working through to the other side of the wall. With God's grace I am working to realign my life and I am focused on God's will. My heart is being instructed and ultimately softened by this experience and related suffering of being in rehab. I believe this experience is a key aspect in my redemptive journey. It broke down my pride, it helped me realign my priorities.

"Reading about Jesus has opened his life to me. I have an enormous joy in my heart for the way this experience has demonstrated that the journey to the cross is an imperative aspect of my walk with Christ."

Answering the question was cathartic. I felt like I was purging myself of my *self*.

After I finished, the room was silent.

"Thank you, Stu," Bob said. "That was one of the best descriptions of the wall I've ever heard."

Then Bob and I looked at the rest of the group, and many were staring at me with tears rolling down their faces.

A Rehab Ministry while Still in Rehab!

When I checked into Lakeside-Milam, I brought my Bible. The people at the front desk, however, objected.

"You are not allowed to bring your Bible into rehab. This isn't a Christian rehab center. We have other books we'd like you to read, including the Alcoholics Anonymous book. Why don't you leave your Bible with your wife?"

"Listen," I answered. "No Bible, no me. I'm checking in voluntarily, and I will be bringing my Bible."

The two women looked at each other and then back at me. "Okay, if you want to bring your Bible, go ahead."

At 5:30 every morning, I poured myself a cup of coffee and sat in the conference room to read my Bible and write in my journal. There was something about being in a setting free of distractions that allowed me to reflect on my growing faith and God's work in my life. My heart was a sponge for God's word. I needed to savor every morsel I read and record how it affected my heart. Finally clean of alcohol for the first time since college, I felt alert and renewed.

Early one morning, after a few days of doing this, a couple of men walked into the conference room.

"What are you doing?" one of them asked.

"Reading my Bible and praying to God."

"If we had a Bible, we'd read and pray with you."

"Come join me," I answered.

Thus began my 5:30 morning Bible study. What started with three men quickly began to grow.

The problem was that we had only one Bible.

Sundays are family days at Lakeside-Milam when we could receive visitors. Trish, Erich, and my Dad would visit me. (Hannah was attending Whitworth University and couldn't visit, but she called me.) My first Sunday when Trish visited me, I told her, "Listen, there are no Bibles in here, so when you come next time, smuggle some Bibles in your purse and I'll give them to the people who are joining me during morning devotion time."

One morning, Deena, a nurse in rehab for addiction to pain killers, walked up to me and said, "You're reading a Bible."

"Yes, I am." I answered.

"Who's this Jesus guy?"

I sort of raised my eyebrows and said, "Well, hey, I'll get you a Bible and we'll talk about Jesus."

Every Sunday during my stay at Lakeside-Milam, Trish smuggled Bibles into the facility. At 5:30 in the morning and then 8:30 every evening, I led a prayer group in the conference room. By the end of my thirty days, as many as twenty people attended out of the ninety patients.

Leading the group came naturally for me. While I understood that I needed to focus on my recovery, I also realized that rehab centers were fertile soil for introducing people to a relationship with Jesus Christ. During our times together, I felt a surge of energy and renewed purpose and began wondering if the next chapter of my life would look more like this.

Every night after we finished, my daily assigned responsibility was to sweep the floors and empty the trash from 9:30 to 10:30 p.m. In God's infinite wisdom, he humbled this proud corporate executive and gave him the most menial job on the floor. It was just what I needed.

After my thirty days were up, the departing patients participated in a formal graduation, and I was asked to say a few words. My speech was pretty simple. I quoted 1 Peter 5:6-11:

> Humble yourselves, therefore, under the mighty hand of God so that at the proper time he may exalt you, casting all your anxieties on him, because he cares for you. Be sober-minded; be watchful. Your adversary the devil prowls around like a roaring lion, seeking someone to devour. Resist him, firm in your faith, knowing that the same kinds of suffering are being experienced by your brotherhood throughout the world. And after you have suffered a little while, the God of all grace, who has called you to his eternal glory in Christ, will himself restore, confirm, strengthen, and establish you. To him be the dominion forever and ever. Amen.

Then my family showed up and helped me check out, and I returned home. Clean and sober, I had never felt better!

I stayed connected to some of the people from rehab and found local AA groups to attend, which supplemented my four-week intensive outpatient care. Then I returned to work at Domaine Selections and within a week I relapsed for the next six weeks.

Relapsing was a very sobering experience for me (pun intended). The four weeks leading up to my fall went so well that I forgot how much work I still needed to do. To minimize the possibility of this happening again, I plugged into an AA meeting and found a sponsor named Mike who helped me walk through the twelve steps.

Every morning I woke up at 4:00 a.m., spent time with God, and then worked on my twelve steps with my sponsor. I attended an AA meeting every day. I also found a Christian recovery program called Celebrate Recovery that I have initiated at various churches, and still lead and attend to this day.

My relapse helped me realize that I couldn't work around wines every day and stay sober. That meant separating myself from Domaine Selections. All our net worth was tied up in the business, but it didn't matter. I could choose sobriety or Domaine Selections. So I met with John and informed him that he would need to run Domaine Selections full-time without my help, which he had been doing for the prior couple of months anyway. It was a difficult conversation and put him in a tough spot. But I needed to do it to remain sober.

December 4, 2010, I finally got sober. I have remained sober ever since. The biggest reason for my success thus far is because Jesus has taken the place of alcohol in my life, and the space he is filling in my heart continues to overcome the temptations of my flesh.

With my internal world coming together, I felt better prepared to take on the SEC.

ELEVEN

TRIALS, TRIBULATIONS, AND REDEMPTION

Securities fraud trial of former Isilon CFO underway

Stuart Fuhlendorf, former chief financial officer of Isilon Systems, who is accused of securities fraud in a civil lawsuit surrounding the company's IPO in 2006, is finally getting his day in court.

Fuhlendorf's jury trial in federal court in Seattle before U.S. District Court Judge Marsha Pechman is underway. In court papers, Fuhlendorf called the allegations in the SEC's lawsuit "severe and highly defamatory" and said the SEC has made "vague, general and sometimes contradictory allegations" that fail to rise to the level of fraud allegations. (*Puget Sound Business Journal,* May 4, 2011)

Twenty months after the SEC filed charges against me, I finally got my day in court.

Although I maintained my innocence throughout the waiting period, the Stuart Fuhlendorf of September 14, 2009, when the charges were filed, was worlds different from the Stuart Fuhlendorf of May 4, 2011.

First of all, I was healthy and six months sober. During my recovery I read in 1 Corinthians 6:19-20 that "Your bodies are temples of the Holy Spirit, who is in you, whom you have received from God. You are not your own; you were bought at a price. Therefore honor God with your bodies" (NIV). This Scripture passage challenged me to take better care of myself, so I began working out and dropped a lot of weight (a total of 108 pounds in two years). The day the trial began, I felt clear minded, healthy, and empowered in my faith in Jesus. This was not the case two years before.

Additionally, I felt strongly that God was at work in my trial and tribulations. The fire of hardship was purifying the gold within, purging me of impurities that tainted my perspective, my marriage, my relationships with my family, and my relationship with Christ. Every day, the words of the apostle Peter burned within me:

> Beloved, do not be surprised at the fiery trial
> when it comes upon you to test you, as though
> something strange were happening to you. But
> rejoice insofar as you share Christ's sufferings,

that you may also rejoice and be glad when his
glory is revealed. (1 Peter 4:12-13)

As I adjusted to living a life of sobriety, I realized I
could no longer work in the wine distribution business
for obvious reasons. This placed a significant strain on my
relationship with my business partner. He understandably
felt abandoned. I read about Joseph in Genesis 39. His
boss's wife tempted him with adultery. Sometimes we
need to confront problems directly; other times we need
to run. Joseph ran away from the temptress. I needed to
run away from my work in the wine business, regardless
of the ramifications.

In my desire to be self-sufficient, I ignored my
weaknesses and danger zones. As a young and growing
believer, I realized that personal autonomy was an illusion.
I needed the power of the Holy Spirit to make healthy
choices—physically, spiritually, and emotionally. I needed
the wisdom that comes only from God.

To his credit, John carried the burdens of our
company amidst the fallout of the Great Recession. Some
of those burdens were the result of debt I pressured us
to take on, debt of which we were both personally liable.
If Domaine Selections went belly-up, the Fuhlendorf net
worth would disappear.

As my self-reliance began to wane, I grew in my
reliance on God, even with the outcome of my upcoming
trial still undetermined. After spending most of my life

relying solely on my ability to outsmart and outhustle everyone around me, this was nothing short of a miracle. *God is in control.* The more I meditated on that simple truth, the more I felt at peace.

But to experience this transformation required God's grace, a reclamation project that called for a complete rebuild. The old was gone; the new had come, as Paul wrote in 2 Corinthians 5:17.

As the defendant, I felt very much out of control in the months preceding the trial. I could refute the allegations on the witness stand, but I couldn't control my lawyers, much less the SEC's lawyers. It didn't help that the *Seattle Business Magazine* published a 2009 article naming me as an example of one of the worst business people in Seattle. How would my lawyers be able to obtain an unbiased jury?

The week before the trial, I read a sermon on the fallacy of self-sufficiency in the Christian life, delivered by my preaching hero Charles Haddon Spurgeon. I kept this paragraph from his sermon in my wallet during the trial:

> The Lord Jesus says [in John 15:5], "Without Me you can do nothing." Strive as you might— struggle as you might—your striving and your struggling would be misapplied strength! They would not speed you towards the goal—they would but sink you deeper into the mire of desperation or of presumption. Mark, further,

the text does not say, "Without Me you can not do some great things—some special acts of piety, some high and supernatural deeds of daring—of self-denial and self-sacrifice." No, "Without Me you can do *nothing*." Including in the sentence, as you will clearly perceive, those little acts of divine grace—those little deeds of piety—for which, perhaps, in our proud self-conceit, we think ourselves to be already sufficiently equipped. You can do *nothing*; not only is the higher duty beyond your power, but the lesser duty, too. You are not capable of performing the lowest act of the divine life, except as you receive strength from God the Holy Spirit!" (C. H. Spurgeon, *Self Sufficiency Slain*, November 11, 1860)

Heading into the trial, Peter and Kurt discussed the possibility of settling out of court. If I admitted guilt, I would be fined millions of dollars—which my directors and officers insurance would cover—and we could avoid the trial. The worst-case scenario would be a lifetime ban from working as a CFO of a publicly traded company, which didn't matter to me.

Nevertheless, I knew I was innocent. Pleading guilty and settling out of court was unacceptable. Just like pleading guilty for a DUI because it was true, I had little interest in pleading guilty for doing something that was untrue. Besides, they told me the government wasn't interested in settling anyway. They were committed to taking me down and making me an example.

Knowing that trials can be risky, Trish asked me if I was emotionally prepared to face a month of proceedings.

"Look," I told her. "If God can give me the strength to go through rehab and stay sober, if he can give me the strength to lose a hundred pounds, then he can give me the strength to make it through the trial."

"Additionally," I told her, "not only has God given me the strength, but Ecclesiastes 7:14 tells me that, 'In the day of prosperity be joyful, and in the day of adversity consider: God has made the one as well as the other.' Clearly, I'm going through this for a reason—for his glory and my good!"

Then I Sensed the Call

After rehab, I started getting involved in Celebrate Recovery, a Christian-based recovery ministry, which led me into a prison ministry through Mars Hill Church. I loved working with the men who were recovering from their addictions while serving time in jail, and in fact, I mentored a few of them. When I started in this ministry, many of the inmates knew more about the Bible than me, but they appreciated that I could relate to their struggles and that I was there because I loved them, and more importantly, that Jesus loved them.

Deeper than that, I felt my heart coming alive as I helped make a difference in the lives of other men. I also found men gravitating toward me for spiritual direction.

In late 2010, I sat down with Trish to discuss our future.

"You know, Trish," I began. "I feel blessed about where God is taking our lives. It's been a struggle, but I can sense that God is leading us as he knocks down each of the moles that keep popping out of the hole. Obviously, Domaine Selections probably isn't going to make it and we're still a few months away from the trial, but my newfound love for Christ isn't going away. I feel a yearning to know God at a deeper and more profound level. I may even want to go to seminary and become a full-time pastor."

Trish just looked at me with a big smile on her face and gave me a bear hug.

"Be careful what you pray for," she said through tears. "I asked God to save my husband. A garden-variety Christian man would have sufficed, but he's giving me a Charles Spurgeon!"

After researching different seminaries, Denver Seminary seemed like the best fit, and best of all, it was located in our home state of Colorado.

Soon, I was accepted into their Master of Divinity program, which would take three or four years to complete. Classes would begin a month after the trial, so we decided to move to Denver a month before the trial. We had sold our home in Woodinville a couple years prior and were renting a house. The owners were interested in selling the house anyway, so they allowed us to break our lease.

After deciding to move, I informed my business partner. He wasn't surprised because I had disengaged from daily operations anyway.

John told me that it was highly likely that Domaine Selections wasn't going to make it, and we might have to unwind it in bankruptcy or simply sell the assets off. It would mean that all the equity and net worth that I had put into Domaine Selections after cashing out the stock options would potentially go away. Same with him, and I felt terrible about it for him, but I knew it was God's will.

Ultimately, the business went under by 2012, and so did my friendship with my dear friend and business partner. John was understanding of my situation. He had seen my life and health spiraling out of control and knew I needed to focus on my recovery and sobriety. My health and spiritual life grew stronger in the years that followed, but that was not the case for our business. The pressures and events that led to its collapse took a toll on our relationship.

Trish and I sat down with Erich and Hannah to inform them of our decision to move back home, knowing full well that they might want to stay in Seattle. They both told us that Seattle was their home, and they would stay. We were blessed beyond belief, when over time, they both changed their minds and moved to Colorado.

So we moved back to the foothills of Colorado in preparation for seminary. Trish didn't have a job. I didn't have a job. We didn't know how we were going to pay the bills, but we knew God was calling us to Denver, and me into full-time pastoral ministry.

While living in Seattle, Trish began working in commercial radio sales. After moving to Denver, she learned that her former boss was working with K-LOVE radio, a nationwide Christian radio network. He created a position with Trish in mind, she applied, and they hired her. It was a huge blessing and provision from God. To help pay the bills on my end while going to school, I landed a ministry position at Mission Hills Church, a large church in the southwest Denver metro area.

Trial by Fire

Leading up to the trial, I focused my time and energy on preparing for court. Surprisingly enough, I felt little stress. Over the previous twenty months, I invested hundreds of hours poring over Isilon documents, reading depositions and transcribed interviews, and meeting with Peter and Kurt. I felt comfortable with the material and grew confident that the SEC was falsely accusing me of fraudulent accounting practices.

If common sense prevailed in the courts, they would throw the case out before it even began. However, knowing the monumental number of hours the SEC already expended on my case, I knew it would go to trial.

According to plan, Trish and I flew back to Seattle for the proceedings. Peter and Kurt told me it would last four weeks in federal court. With outstanding lawyers representing me, they advised me to sit still and then tell the truth when it was my turn to testify.

On May 4, as the foreman called everyone to rise and Judge Marsha Pechman entered the room, I still felt an overwhelming sense of peace.

John Yuen, the lead prosecuting attorney for the Securities and Exchange Commission, began by calling an Isilon salesperson to the stand. After giving his name, the first witness recounted his version of how I coordinated the side deal. And so began the argument that I was "cooking the books."

While I understood that the Isilon salespeople were protecting themselves, Trish struggled to sit in her seat and listen. At times when I was CFO of Isilon I would occasionally speak with a few salespeople or their boss on the phone while at home in the evening or on the weekend. Trish knew some of the salespeople and accountants in the company and had overheard the conversation the first witness was describing, and it was not at all how she remembered it. The testimony was a complete fabrication. Livid, she begged my lawyers to let her take the stand and testify, but they said no. They knew the jury would consider her testimony biased.

The second salesperson was an uncomfortable witness. He struggled answering the questions to the satisfaction of the prosecuting attorney. The third was even more uncomfortable than the second. It was clear the SEC was trying to extract incriminating evidence from Isilon employees that wasn't there. Some deals may have been improperly accounted for given the vast number of deals negotiated by the salespeople, but the SEC was having a hard time connecting that I had any knowledge of the details of the deals.

Leading up to the trial, Trish and I discussed some of the salespeople and the deals in question. In retrospect, it would have been easier for her to simply support her husband without knowing the facts.

Various salespeople in the company testified, some of whom I hardly knew because they lived and worked around the world. One of them recounted detailed "conversations" that was nothing short of implausible. After the court recessed for the day, we walked out of the building at the same time as the salesperson who lied that afternoon on the witness stand. Trish was so angry I thought she would confront the man with a verbal take-down and a flying tackle. Fortunately, she restrained herself, but she glared at him for being the lying, self-protecting scoundrel that he was.

I, on the other hand, felt overwhelming gratitude for being healthy and sober. A peace beyond all understanding. Listening to the false accusations, I felt a deep connection to the apostles in the Bible and saints throughout history who were persecuted. They suffered for their righteous faith in Jesus Christ as their Lord and Savior. My suffering was not for righteousness sake, but I yearned for it in the future. Some days during the trial, I even daydreamed about suffering for Christ rather than worldly matters. Our mutual suffering became a connecting point between me, Christ, and his first-century followers.

If anything, God used the trial to cleanse me and prepare me for seminary. In a blessed and mysterious sort of way, it was exactly what I needed.

During the four-week trial, I could see God intervening on my behalf. For instance, John Yuen, called one salesperson to the stand.

"What did Mr. Fuhlendorf tell you to do?" Yuen asked.

"He told me to book the deal even though there was a return provision," the salesperson answered. That was the crux of his testimony and a lie. But just as he began, a courthouse speaker started blaring throughout the building. The loud, garbled voice sounded like a PA system on a New York subway where you can barely understand what the conductor is saying. This *loud* distraction completely drowned out his answer.

In the midst of the interruption, Trish and I looked at each other and then she mouthed, "That was God!" I nodded and smiled.

Afterward, Judge Pechman looked out in astonishment and told everyone in the courthouse, "That has never happened at any time while I have sat on the bench in this building." He later repeated his testimony, but it lacked the impact of his first attempt.

Sitting in the courtroom, listening to my character being pummeled was demoralizing. Then, at the end of the first week, I endured another blow to my pride: I still needed to serve time for my DUI.

Onward and Downward

Friday afternoon, as the court recessed for the weekend, Trish and I walked back to the Westin Hotel. The next morning, I checked myself in to the King County Jail. Enduring a long week listening to the United States government's false accusations and then telling the taxi cab driver to drive me to the King County Jail so I could spend the next twenty-four hours behind bars was a bit surreal to say the least. Trish spent the evening with friends.

Only one week down, three to go.

Coming off my lovely weekend accommodations, staying positive was a challenge. But God sent me a reminder that he was present in the purifying fire.

Halfway through the second week of testimony by forensic accounting experts, stock price valuation consultants, and various employees and Isilon board members, including the controller and chairman of the Audit Committee, I glanced at one of the jury members. He smiled at me and nodded. I took it as an expression of support and felt engulfed in God's peace.

At other times, the trial was truly a battle of faith and endurance. In the early days of the trial during a side session with John Yuen and Peter Ehrlichman, Judge Pechman commented with a bite of sarcasm, "Well, I can't imagine why we're going through this trial if this man (she then pointed at me) *isn't* guilty."

Peter blew up. He objected to her comment in a red-faced tirade. Risking a contempt of court charge, he threatened to file for a mistrial if the judge had already presumed his client's guilt.

Though I always felt supported by my great team of lawyers, I felt some despair that Judge Pechman's attitude about my guilt would influence the jury. "What's the point," I thought, "if they already think I'm guilty?"

The SEC lawyers stayed in the same hotel as Trish and me. We avoided each other the best we could, but one day I ran into the hotel elevator where John Yuen was standing alone. The doors closed, and there I stood before my accuser.

At that moment, Proverbs 25:21-22 popped into my head: "If your enemy is hungry, give him bread to eat, and if he is thirsty, give him water to drink, for you will heap burning coals on his head, and the LORD will reward you."

I looked at John, smiled pleasantly, and complimented him with all sincerity. "John, I think you are a superb lawyer. I've been very impressed with your courtroom demeanor and the quality in which you've represented the government."

John mumbled, "Thank you," while staring at the ground. When the elevator doors opened, he scurried out as fast as he could.

My Day in Court Finally Arrived

Apart from that first weekend, Trish and I spent the weekends back in Denver for a respite from the proceedings.

Midway through the trial, my time for examination and cross-examination arrived. Peter and Kurt told me they expected it to last three days. I felt well-prepared and at peace knowing I had the truth on my side.

Four hours into his questioning, John Yuen looked down at his pad of paper and began flipping through his notes. The way he looked down at his notepad reminded me of the way he looked down at the ground when he responded to me on the elevator. He was troubled. Then he made the most astonishing comment of the trial—at least as far as I was concerned.

"No more questions, your honor."

I couldn't believe my ears. Trish and I locked eyes and smiled. This was going better than I ever expected. Judge Pechman recessed the trial until the next day.

The next morning Peter stood up and began his cross-examination of me. The master litigator began asking me questions that were convincing and on point. I answered honestly and sincerely. As the questions and answers continued, it became clear that my legal

team felt satisfied with the way my testimony was
proceeding.

Finally, Peter looked at the judge and said, "No more
questions, your honor."

"You may take your seat, Mr. Fuhlendorf," Judge
Pechman said.

I spent ten hours on the witness stand—when
I expected *at least* three days. I felt so prepared for
questioning that, to be honest, I was a little disappointed
to take my seat.

The SEC attorneys knew they had their hands full
because the truth was on my side.

Finally, when Peter concluded the defense, the
case went to jury. Peter and Kurt explained that the
deliberations could take a while but assured me that the
trial was a success. The judge gave us permission to fly
home while we waited for the verdict. Time would tell
what the jury thought.

Then We Waited

The threshold for conviction in a civil case is normally
lower than a criminal case. The majority decision would
prevail. However, due to the magnitude of the accusations,
the judge instructed the jury that only a unanimous
decision in favor or against me would prevail. The judge's
instructions about the verdict requiring a unanimous
decision could work for me or against me.

While I waited for the verdict, I received an encouraging e-mail from a member of my legal team. It is a note that I still keep in my office desk. It said:

Dear Stu,

I wanted you to know that I have been involved in various matters of law and litigation over the years. Please know that regardless of the outcome of your case your sense of peace, grace and gentleness during the trial has been an inspiration to me. You are different than others whom I've served in practice. I gather that it is the work of God in your life.

I yearn to have what you have.

After a week, my lawyers called me with the outcome of the trial.

"I have good news," Peter said, his voice unable to hide his excitement. "It's a hung jury. The jury couldn't reach a unanimous verdict, so the charges will probably be dropped."

"Given the weak evidence, we don't see how the SEC would retry your case," Kurt added. "So go celebrate . . . within reason, of course."

"Gentlemen," I started. Overcome with emotion, I needed a few moments to regain my composure before I continued. "I can't thank you enough. Both of you have been a gift from God to both Trish and me. I'll always feel indebted to you for your support, encouragement, and expertise."

We hung up the phone and then Trish and I celebrated . . . within reason, of course.

Later, I discovered that the majority of jurors ruled in my favor. I also learned that some of the SEC attorneys, particularly a female lawyer who really bugged Trish, were in tears over the verdict.

While the proceedings tarnished my character, Isilon moved forward as a successful business, although it took a hit on the street for not supporting one of their own.

In the year prior to the trial, they offered me a check for $120,000 if I would indemnify them against me suing them in the future. I took the money and signed the indemnification document. I was becoming a different person every day because my old self would have sued the pants off of them. We used the money to pay off some debts and poured the rest of it into Domaine Selections in an attempt to keep the business afloat.

Most disappointing to me, though, was that after all those years, no one from the company—not a board member, outside auditor, or my replacement—asked me about any of the deals in question, or ever received any input from me about any of the matters.

Moving forward, Peter and Kurt felt that the SEC knew they had a weak case and would not retry it. They were wrong. Just a few weeks after the conclusion of the trial, the SEC informed them they would retry my case. Seminary would be starting in a few weeks, and I told Peter and Kurt that they would have to try the case without me sitting at the defendant's table.

Peter and Kurt were incredulous at this notion. They immediately hopped on a plane to Colorado to convince me otherwise. I stuck to my guns, so they decided to play a game of bluff with the SEC. They told the SEC that we eagerly wanted to move forward with the retrial. In the eleventh hour, the SEC reached out to Peter to inform him that they would not retry.

After all the time, money, and effort, the only thing the government could glean out of their hard work and destruction of my reputation was my agreement not to be a CFO for a few years, which didn't fit into God's plans for me anyway. No conviction. No financial settlement. No admittance of guilt.

With the court case behind me, I could now enter my next season of life sober, healthy, and *free*! It didn't matter that we didn't have much money because Domaine Selections was preparing to unwind in bankruptcy.

Through the walk to sobriety, SEC trial, bankruptcy, the loss of our Woodway property—the loss of nearly everything, really—God dealt with my pride and self-sufficiency. That's why I can look back at the hardship without any bitterness.

I still stumble and fall. The desire for autonomy still tempts me. Nevertheless, with God's help, I can continue growing in my trust in him.

My life would take on a magnified sense of purpose and meaning from this point forward.

Securities fraud trial of ex-Isilon CFO ends with hung jury

A federal jury in Seattle was not able to reach a verdict in the SEC's civil trial against Stuart Fuhlendorf, the former chief financial officer of Isilon Systems accused of securities fraud.

After deliberations that started May 6, the SEC wound up with a hung jury Wednesday in the case, according to a clerk in U.S. District Court Judge Marsha Pechman's office. (*Puget Sound Business Journal*, May 11, 2011)

EPILOGUE

A week or two after the smoke cleared from the trial, I sat on the deck of our rented home in Genesee Park, Colorado. With the SEC lawsuit behind me and nearly all of our net worth gone, my previous life in corporate America seemed like a distant memory.

I felt free. Free from the wrongful accusations. Free from alcohol abuse. A total reboot.

"Lord," I prayed. "What's next?"

I reflected on the Samaritan woman at the well in John 4. Like her, I knew that Jesus revealed himself to me not because I was good or smart or even worthy and deserving. He revealed himself to me because he loved me. Because he chose me.

Living life on my terms—the definition of self-sufficiency—only brought heartache and pain. Yet I wasn't bitter.

Sitting on our deck, I read Hebrews 12:25: "See that you do not refuse him who is speaking." As I read this verse over and over again, I pondered my journey from Wall Street to seminary. Most of my life I pursued my dreams of building a business and making as much money as possible. I didn't want to believe in God because I didn't want anything to get in the way of those dreams or anybody to tell me what to do.

In other words, I refused to listen to "him who is speaking."

Reading further in Hebrews 12, the writer tells us:

> At that time his voice shook the earth, but now he has promised, "Once more I will shake not only the earth but also the heavens." The words "once more" indicate the removing of what can be shaken—that is, created things— so that what cannot be shaken may remain. (Hebrews 12:26-27, NIV)

Suddenly, a light went on in my mind. Because I refused him who speaks, he shook not only the earth but the heavens. In his great love for me, God shook my world. He allowed my life to reach the brink of self-destruction in order to get my attention, cleanse my life, and redeem it. He separated me from the distractions— my possessions, my desire for adulation, my fixation on me—that prevented me from surrendering to him.

I realized that everything I built apart from him was shakable. Like a rigid house ill-equipped to survive an earthquake, the edifices we build as monuments to us will crumble when God begins to shake them.

God, on the other hand, is a master builder. Everything he builds will remain. Unshakable.

The writer of Hebrews completes his thought with this:

Therefore, since we are receiving a kingdom that cannot be shaken, let us be thankful, and so worship God acceptably with reverence and awe, for our "God is a consuming fire." (Hebrews 12:28-29, NIV)

Feelings of joy overwhelmed me in that moment. "God, thank you for the wounds you faithfully inflicted on me," I prayed. "Through them you revealed yourself to me and my utter need for you."

It is this purging of worldly things from our lives that makes us holier and pares away the influences that come between us and him. He used my suffering for his purpose and my good.

I lost much, but I gained so much more in return.

From Then Until Now

In June of 2011, I began classes at Denver Seminary with a heart on fire for God—and my classes only fanned the flame. I didn't know what I wanted to do after grad school, but I knew my studies would give me a better sense of God's calling on my life and Trish's life with me.

While Trish worked at K-LOVE, I dove headfirst into an exploration of theology and God's character. Like a puzzle, pieces of my story began making sense. Perhaps God allowed me to go through the pain and frustration of my SEC lawsuit and bankruptcy, so I could gain a better understanding of people in their suffering. While not the cause of it, perhaps God allowed me to experience the effects of alcohol addiction, so I could gain a better understanding of those who struggle with addictions, who walk through rehab, even spend time in prison.

My second year in seminary I sensed a strong call from God to become a pastor, working full-time for God's kingdom both inside and outside the church. One of my seminary professors gave me the name of a young associate pastor at Mission Hills Church. Josh Weidman became a friend and mentor. Then Pastor Josh offered me an intern position working at the church for eight dollars an hour. *Some years earlier, I was worth $10 million on paper.*

I couldn't have been happier!

Soon, Pastor Josh and Mike Romberger, the senior pastor, offered me a full-time ministry position. Trish and I also started a Celebrate Recovery ministry at Mission Hills. With Pastor Josh, I helped lead the creation of the Care and Crisis Counseling Center. The more I served, the more I grew in my love for the Lord and the more I knew God had called me to pastoral ministry. Mission Hills eventually hired me as their pastor of evangelism and outreach, where I led the local and international mission teams and the development of the Mission Hills Community Life Center.

After graduating from Denver Seminary in 2015, I reflected again on Hebrews 12:25, "See that you do not refuse him who is speaking."

"God," I prayed. "How are you speaking to me? Where are you leading me?"

After a great deal of prayer, I sensed God leading me to serve in a local church as a senior pastor. So in January 2016, I resigned from Mission Hills, and without a job or much money, I began interviewing with churches.

Through it all, God led me to a small, growing church in suburban Littleton, Colorado, called Redemption Hills, where I enjoy preaching, ministering, and partnering with God as he builds the church. We're a Bible-believing, Christ-focused church with a vision of transformational evangelism, discipleship, and mission that shares the love of Jesus with people in need.

Self-Sufficiency or Christ-Sufficiency?

I have a friend who is known for saying, "You will never know that Jesus is all you need, until Jesus is all you have." The opposite of self-sufficiency is Christ-sufficiency. For me, the foundation of Christ-sufficiency is the pursuit of total surrender to his will and not my own.

I pray often that God will always keep some significant unmet need in my life so that I'm always dependent on him. To be surrendered and in need creates dependency on him. Having too much creates self-sufficiency. When our lives prosper, the natural tendency is to lose our grip on him.

Someone once called this prayer courageous, but it is not. It's a prayer of fear and awe—awe of a holy God. For

God has the power to give us what we deserve, whether good or bad. I have come to fear, with reverence and awe, the God who is, for he is a consuming fire.

To be Christ-sufficient doesn't mean that we surrender our minds, but our wills. To surrender the will doesn't diminish the intellect. Just the opposite, the sharpened mind leads us through the process of surrender. Only thinking people advance themselves, either toward self-sufficiency or Christ-sufficiency.

Jesus' words in 2 Corinthians 12:9 are comforting, "My grace is sufficient for you, for my power is made perfect in weakness." Christ may or may not ask you to change your lifestyle, as he did me, but he does command you to surrender it to him, and to do so regularly.

I've learned to never hold back in areas that Jesus reveals are un-surrendered. Holding back leads to self-sufficiency and results in a scuffling with the process of daily surrender. We are converted to faith in a moment of surrender, like my experience in London that night in 2006, but we are converted to obedience and being Christ-sufficient over a lifetime by surrendering to him anew daily. First comes the moment of surrender, then comes the process of becoming Christ-sufficient.

Jesus says as much in Luke 9:23. "If anyone would come after me, he must deny himself and take up his cross daily and follow me." The power of Christ-sufficiency is that it's no longer about you! Now, in God's eyes, it *is* about you. That's why he sent Jesus to die for your sins. But from our perspective, it's no longer about us.

Paul wrote in Galatians 2:20: "I have been crucified with Christ. It is no longer I who live, but Christ who lives in me. And the life I now live in the flesh I live by faith in the Son of God, who loved me and gave himself for me."

When we yield our lives to Christ, our fleshly lives die, and Christ lives through us. Our past no longer matters because it's been forgiven. Romans 8:1 tells us, "There is therefore now no condemnation for those who are in Christ Jesus." Your past doesn't matter to God!

That's good news for us because all of us are no better than the Samaritan woman at the well. Beating ourselves up over our past is actually an act of pride because it tells Jesus, "Your death on the cross to forgive my sin was not enough! My sins are more powerful than your ability to forgive." The embodiment of self-sufficiency!

Believe me, I still wrestle with guilt and shame over my past and current behaviors. Then I repent and remind myself that King David was an adulterer and the apostle Paul murdered Christians.

We *all* need Jesus!

The Holy Spirit has shown me that only through our past mistakes, our past sins, our tribulations and sufferings can we gain a greater understanding and empathy for the struggles of others. More important, they give us an understanding of the suffering and struggles of Christ on the cross.

The following Scripture passage is tattooed on my shoulder.

Resist him [referring to Satan], standing firm in the faith, because you know that the family of believers throughout the world is undergoing the same kind of sufferings. And the God of all grace, who called you to his eternal glory in Christ, after you have suffered a little while, will himself restore you and make you strong, firm and steadfast. To him be the power for ever and ever. Amen. (1 Peter 5:9-11, NIV)

When I stand firm in my faith in the Lord, I know that in everything, God has a purpose for me, all the way from Wall Street to the well. My sufferings, then, will restore, confirm, strengthen, and establish me for God's good. It's the same for you if you have faith in Jesus Christ as your Lord and Savior. It's a truth that never fades.

It's all for his glory—from Wall Street to the glory. To him be the dominion and power forever and ever, amen.

ABOUT THE AUTHOR

STU FUHLENDORF is the senior pastor of Redemption Hills Church in Littleton, Colorado. After spending the first half of his career in the competitive world of high-tech software and systems development as a business executive, Stu spends much of his time studying,  preaching, and teaching the gospel to those with unique challenges in life and a need for Jesus—namely all of us. Stu is being used as a servant of God in ministry to help men and women think more deeply about their lives and overcome the devastating effects of idol worship, addictions, and sin in a suffering world.

Through his studies, speaking, and writings he has become a tireless advocate for men and women, encouraging and inspiring them to change their lives in Christ and teaching the gospel in a committed fashion. Stu often reflects on his own experiences in biblical terms as he participates regularly at various prison ministries, redemption ministries for those recently released from prison, street ministries, and recovery ministries. He is regularly invited to preach and speak at churches and conferences nationwide.

He has served on the board of directors of the School of Business and Leadership at Colorado Christian University and the foundation board of the University of Northern Colorado, in addition to other profit and nonprofit boards.

Stu earned a master of divinity (MDiv) from the Denver Seminary, a master of business administration (MBA) from the University of San Diego, and a bachelor of arts (BA) in social science education from the University of Northern Colorado.

He lives in Indian Hills, Colorado, with his wife, Trish. They have two grown children who divide their time between school, work, and fun in Colorado.

Go to www.WallStreetToTheWell.com for more information.